COLLECTING
ORIENTAL RUGS

Joyce C. Ware
Line drawings by Wilson P. Ware

HOUSE OF COLLECTIBLES
NEW YORK

Instant Expert: Collecting Oriental Rugs

by Joyce C. Ware

Copyright © 2004 by Random House, Inc.

Library of Congress Cataloging-in-Publication Data is available.

First Edition

0 9 8 7 6 5 4 3 2 1

May 2004

ISBN: 0-375-72044-8

CONTENTS

PART 3: THE COLLECTIBLE RUG MARKET

This guide is dedicated to Leslie O'Grady and Sharon Schulze, critique partners par excellence.

ACKNOWLEDGMENTS

Information and gossip about the current rug market was generously shared with me by American Conference on Oriental Rugs stalwarts Charles Lave, Bethany Mendenhall, and Mark Hopkins and *HALI*'s affable editor, Daniel Shaffer.

I am greatly indebted to Peter Pap, George Jevremovic, Bill McDonnell, Can Gurel, John Collins, Paul Ramsey, and Gayle Garrett for the loan of color transparencies and/or the permission to download images from their websites.

Jo Kris, the rug expert at Skinner, Inc., the notably user-friendly auction house in Boston, supplied me with recent rug sales catalogs and permission to use images from them.

Special thanks are due to Dorothy Harris, my editor, Lindsey Glass, her unflappable assistant, Fabrizio La Rocca, Random House's creative director, and last, but far from least, Arthur Coates, my talented son, who set up the Microsoft Excel spreadsheet I needed for the book's art log.

INTRODUCTION

The wide variety of knotted-pile and flat-woven textiles that originated in Turkey (Anatolia), Iran (Persia), Afghanistan, the Caucasus, Turkestan, East Central Asia, India, China, and Egypt are known collectively as "oriental rugs." Beautiful weavings are still being produced in these areas, and Romania now produces pile rugs in addition to its distinctive floral-patterned kilims.

Genuine oriental rugs are made by hand. Well-designed machine-made rugs like the American-made Karastan are superior to carpets printed with oriental-type patterns, but both fall far short of the real thing. Compared to paintings and sculpture, which are commonly classified as "fine art," textiles are an undervalued medium, and the recession that began with the bursting of the technology bubble has adversely affected bids received at auction for decorative arts more than it has the fine arts.

For those seeking a rug as an element of an already planned color scheme, the faded look of unstable dyes or the untraditional palette of a computer-designed carpet may be just what the decorator ordered. If your interest in rugs begins and ends with the desire to own a few attractive pieces, this guide will help you accomplish that straightforward goal. But even though practicality may dictate the use of good new reproductions on a connoisseur's heavily used floor areas, a choice antique collectible rug is a work of textile art as worthy of wall space as a fine painting. If you are anxious to learn what will transform you from an average rug buyer to a collector knowledgeable enough to choose the best rug you can afford, what follows should help you steer clear of the pitfalls awaiting the unwary novice.

The majority of oriental rugs offered for sale at retail stores and at auctions are neither antique nor collectible, and although the terms are sometimes thought synonymous, the growing number of quality reproductions knotted with hand-spun wool and dyed with rich vegetable colors are more worthy of collection than century-old rugs dyed with unstable or garish synthetic colors.

But no one wants to pay antique-rug prices for a copy, no matter how fine it may be. Buy from a reputable dealer. You will find names and sources in the Resource Guide in the back of this guide. Confine your auction forays to the previews, and above all, avoid those widely advertised weekend distress sales held at motels and hotels, where rugs unable to be sold in standard retail outlets are hawked by glib con artists long gone by Monday morning.

Some prominent dealers who limit their offerings to superior collectible rugs are, for the first time, advertising significant reductions in prices. Collectors planning to sell some of their fine old pieces are biding their time until the market settles, and dealers who used to shun new rugs are now stocking the best of the new natural-dye rugs mentioned earlier.

The first hard lesson collectors in any field of the arts learn is that the coveted object bought today, perhaps excitingly vied for at auction, is worth only what the next buyer will pay. In other words, buying rugs primarily for investment is a risky business best left to venture capitalists. That said, please take the following to heart:

1. Since many collectors value age above other attributes, the dating of a rug is often a matter of heated debate. Major auction houses like Sotheby's and Christie's consider rugs as antiques only if they can be safely assumed to be a hundred or more years old. Scholars are reluctant to apply that label to rugs made after the introduction of synthetic dyes, which in some areas was as early as 1870. Many reputable dealers pronounce a rug antique at eighty years of age, semiantique if it predates 1960, and "old" if made at least twenty-five years ago. Disreputable dealers often try to pass off new rugs physically altered and chemically treated to appear old as antiques.

2. World-class collectible rugs boasting exceptional color, design, and condition are expensive. Very occasionally, one is found at a bargain price at a tag sale, antique shop, or rural auction, but these are rare exceptions. Be realistic about what you can afford to spend and adjust your sights accordingly. When tempted to spend beyond one's limit, Joseph Alsop's cogent observation in *The Rare Art Traditions* is worth recalling, "The line between 'worth having' and 'not worth having' is always shifting, since collectors with limited means are constantly exploring all the things 'not worth having' for possible prizes when a new collecting category finds favor."

3. If your busy schedule allows little time for visiting museum collections and attending rug exhibitions and auction previews, put yourself in the hands of a reputable dealer. Those wishing to progress beyond the novice stage must take the time to see the colors, feel the wool, and examine patterns and structures, preferably in the company of knowledgeable collectors. In short, you have to develop an eye. Beautiful pictures are no more than useful accessories.

4. Novice collectors are sometimes hard put to choose the run-of-the-mill over the downright awful. As your

eye improves, you will be able to distinguish good rugs from the ordinary, and in time, the best from the good. But until that happy day arrives, proceed with caution. Buy only those rugs that genuinely please you and be prepared to make mistakes. Anyone who boasts about never having made one is most likely lying. Don't blame yours on the dealer who "talked me into it," the catalog description, inadequate light, or auction fever. The decision was yours. Learn from it.

PART 1:
AN INTRODUCTION
TO ORIENTAL RUGS

1

FIRST THINGS FIRST

An Overview of Rug History and Today's Market

Given the perishability of rug-making materials, a finely knotted carpet with realistic pictorial motifs found in 1949 in eastern Siberia and originally dated between the fifth and third centuries B.C. is considered prima facie proof that the art of knotted-pile textiles must have been well developed by that early date. A bit of Egyptian tapestry weave has been dated to 1450 B.C. and a clay fragment impressed with patterns associated with woven textiles was found in a 27,000-year-old dig in what is now the Czech Republic.

The invasion of Egypt by Islamic armies in A.D. 640 and the North African Moorish domination of Spain from the eighth to the fifteenth centuries influenced the arts in both regions. In Egypt, the distinctively patterned, iridescent fifteenth- and sixteenth-century Mamluk carpets display stylistic links to both Anatolian and northwest Persian weaving of the same period. Curvilinear designs were introduced after the occupation of Cairo by Ottoman Turks in 1517.

Early Spanish carpets reflect the Islamic tradition, except for the custom of knotting the crests of noble families into the carpets commissioned by them. Anatolian influences are seen later, and still later, in the sixteenth and seventeenth centuries, European Baroque patterns were adapted. Although superb early Spanish and Egyptian carpets may be seen in museum collections, and are worth a trip to do so, they are rarely available on the market.

The art of rug weaving reached its peak during the Persian Safavid dynasty (1499–1722). Woven and knotted textiles, indeed all the arts, attained a virtuosity during this period that has never been surpassed. The carpets woven in court workshops were designed by master artists, and highly skilled weavers were allowed to take as much time as was necessary to reproduce with warp, weft, and knotted wool the delicacy of ornament and rich coloration the elegant designs demanded.

In India, the Mughal dynasty workshops produced splendid carpets during the same period. According to the Islamic scholar Walter Denny, "The art was borrowed [from Persia], but as with the Japanese and baseball, it was taken up with enthusiasm. Indian rugs of the classical period are the largest, most finely knotted, and most brilliantly colored carpets ever made."

Typically, these early Indian carpets have glowing claret red grounds patterned with beautifully drawn floral motifs more realistic than those on their Persian models, accompanied by bizarre, wholly unrealistic animals. Except for its distinctive flat-woven dhurries, Indian weaving later became entirely dominated by Persian designs, and its sizable contemporary production consists largely of well-made Persian knockoffs.

Rug weaving in Anatolia, which encompassed much of modern-day Turkey, has a well-established history due to the custom of presenting rugs to mosques as tokens of piety and thanks for blessings received. Over the centuries, these rugs accumulated layer by layer, awaiting discovery by scholars and carefully supervised removal to Turkish museums for documentation and conservation. The earliest of these carpets, large coarse weavings with repeat patterns and strikingly bold border motifs, have been attributed to the Seljuk dynasty (thirteenth to fourteenth centuries). Later, the Ottoman court preferred carpets with elaborate curvilinear floral designs woven with silk and fine wool.

The arched prayer rug has been a popular format throughout Turkey, from the incredibly finely knotted Hereke silks and refined village rugs like the tulip-decorated Ladiks, to the charming, brightly colored, and relatively coarsely knotted geometrized designs produced by the thousands on cottage looms.

Venetian merchants began importing rugs from the Middle East as early as the fourteenth century, first from Anatolia, and later from the Russian Caucasus, where an active cottage industry produced carpets with unique large-scale floral and so-called dragon designs. European fascination with these exotic luxury goods is confirmed by their frequent use as props in the paintings of the period. In fact, the names of two artists, Lorenzo Lotto and Hans Holbein, have been applied to the designs of the Anatolian weavings they most favored, which are used as table covers as often as floor coverings.

A decline in court carpet production in the eighteenth century was an inevitable result of frequent hostile invasions in both Persia and Anatolia. Rulers threatened with toppled thrones had little time for aesthetics. But since village and nomadic life was more concerned with local harvest and pasturage than with the troubles of distant courts, their need for sturdy woven goods remained constant. The rugs, animal and tent trappings, and storage bags produced during this period in remote stone villages and the black tents of nomads are of particular interest to today's collectors because of their motifs' intimate association with the tribal beliefs and family interests of the weavers.

As one travels east from East Turkestan to China, the look of antique rugs gradually differs from those most Westerners think of as oriental. East Turkestan weavers borrowed colors, designs, and motifs from rug-making neighbors both to the east and the west. Tibetan rugs, a Chinese-influenced craft of more recent date, have a unique structure and vigorous designs, among them the well-known tiger rugs.

Until recently, the sparse use of unfamiliar motifs and the typically subdued palette of old Chinese rugs failed to appeal to Western tastes long focused on the brilliantly colored curvilinear floral patterns associated with the term "oriental." Although pile rugs were being made in China as early as the twelfth century, they weren't introduced to Western markets until about 1900, and it is only within the last twenty-five years that sophisticated collectors learned to appreciate the subtle artistry and wonderfully lustrous wool of antique pieces that have nothing in common with the slick, sculptured candy-box prettiness typical of China's vast contemporary production.

Thanks largely to Western painters who became fascinated by the exotic scenes encountered in the Middle East during travels abroad in the latter half of the nineteenth century, European and American interest in oriental carpets took a new lease on life in the wake of exhibitions featuring their canvases. The basis of many stellar museum holdings were acquired just before and after the turn of the twentieth century, but when this revival of interest filtered down to the comfortable middle class, it gave rise to a new and unhappy development. Traditional sizes, colors, and patterns were altered to meet the tastes and furnishing needs of hordes of unsophisticated buyers, and the well-intended quality controls demanded by Western importers resulted in a standardized product entirely lacking in artistic integrity.

It was this development, which continues to this day, that fostered an intense interest in tribal weavings made solely for domestic use and whose designs retained a vigor uninfluenced by Western tastes well into the twentieth century. Although the current unrest in the Middle East has hampered research, collectors who specialize in this field are as interested in the materials, design sources, and day-to-day lives of these tribal people as they are in the beautiful textiles they weave.

The cheap, garish, and easy-to-use synthetic dyes imported from Europe in the late nineteenth and early twentieth centuries nearly destroyed the worldwide cottage weaving industry, principally in Turkey. Fortunately, the reintroduction of vegetable dyes and hand-spun lanolin-rich wool in a group of Turkish village weaving cooperatives in the early 1980s spurred a very well-received wide-ranging revival of beautiful, traditionally dyed woven and patterned rugs that many collectors find a more practical choice for covering floors than fine antiques.

Beginning Your Collection

Perhaps you bought this book hoping to acquire sufficient information to guide the purchase of two or three nice old rugs to complement the colors of already chosen upholstery and window treatments. If so, you will have an easier time negotiating the ins and outs of the oriental rug trade than collectors, but choices limited by an existing scheme are in no way less deserving of serious consideration. No matter what your reason may be for choosing to buy an oriental rug, one maxim always applies: look before you leap.

A careful reading of at least one of the following three books and a subscription to *HALI*, the internationally acclaimed bimonthly guide to carpet, textile, and Islamic art, should precede visits to museum collections, auction previews, and dealers' stocks:

- M. L. Eiland Jr. and M. Eiland III, *Oriental Carpets: A Complete Guide*, 4th ed. (Boston 1998), an essential book for serious collectors

- P. J. R. Ford, *Oriental Carpet Design: A Guide to Traditional Motifs, Patterns, and Symbols* (New York 1992)

- Jon Thompson, *Carpets from the Tents, Cottages and Workshops of Asia* (London 1993)

- *HALI*, www.subscription.co.uk/haliandapg/3016

These should be the cornerstones of your rug book library. As you explore the possibilities, you may find yourself returning again and again to bold geometrically patterned rugs very unlike the elegant floral Persian rugs you originally had in mind. If the attraction is strong enough, you are likely to seek out more and more of the same type in pile rugs, flat weaves, and eventually trappings. An extensive annotated list of recommended titles is included in the Resource Guide. One caution: don't settle for long outdated volumes gathering dust in your local library. The novice rug collector should start with currently recognized authorities. *HALI* publishes articles by scholars and experienced collectors, reports of auctions and exhibitions both here and abroad, rug book reviews, and schedules of upcoming events. The full-color illustrations are a joy to behold and, unlike most periodicals, so are the advertisements placed by dealers and auction houses.

The earliest of the many books devoted to oriental rugs as an art form were published in costly limited editions authored by wealthy collectors. The dealers who sold them their rugs were happy to supply these patrons with off-the-cuff romantic tales about provenance, giving rise to enduring myths still being told by dealers more interested in intriguing potential rug buyers than in relaying accurate information. Factual documentation was either unreliable or altogether lacking.

Fortunately, rug research has made vast strides in the last thirty years. Dealers specializing in antique and collectible weavings are willing to spend time educating new buyers—after all, their business depends on repeat customers—and a well-read novice will soon know a lot more about old rugs than a dealer who stocks only new ones. The best of the scholarly books are expensive, particularly those with many color plates, but there is also a gratifying number of modestly priced, competently written, well-illustrated guides.

Choosing an Area of Concentration

Once you progress beyond the point of thinking of all old oriental rugs as Persian, you will begin to realize the true size and complexity of the collecting field you have chosen to enter. Faced with a bewildering variety of beautiful weavings, it is tempting to adopt the one of this, one of that, assorted-chocolates approach. But unless one is lucky enough to possess an eye able to discriminate quickly between synthetic and natural colors, a wiser course is to continue reading about and looking at rugs until a particular type of weaving consistently appeals to you more than others. It could be the technical excellence of the weaving or the patterns, motifs, and palette typical of a given district. Taken to the extreme, some collectors look only for variations of tree-of-life designs; others confine their search to flat weaves typical of Baluch tribes.

Many collectors buy good weavings from areas other than their chosen specialty when the price is right, but unless one has a great deal of time to devote to viewing, researching, and handling rugs, it is impossible to learn enough about all classes of weavings to unerringly discern not only the good examples, but also the out-of-the-ordinary prizes.

The annotated sales catalogs of the major auction houses provide structural descriptions that are useful to review while inspecting the real thing at the sale's preview. Although their accuracy is sometimes questioned by dealers and scholars, they are of considerable benefit to the average collector. Identifying weave patterns in the quiet of one's home is one thing; attempting it at crowded auction previews is another thing altogether, which is why limiting one's collecting focus is the best way to minimize confusion.

Identification

Beginning collectors tend to identify a rug from its design. If the rug is a traditional type of respectable age—say, eighty years—and one is willing to settle for a general rather than specific identification, the odds for making a reasonably good choice are pretty good. Unfortunately, rugs woven to satisfy the demands of late nineteenth- and early twentieth-century commercial interests are quite another story, since the wool, dyes, and designs supplied by European and American rug importers often had little to do with the weavers' native culture. Even isolated village and tribal weavers unaffected by commercialization were sometimes influenced by the "foreign" motifs seen on rugs brought to regional markets by weavers from other districts.

Authorities advise that given this widespread transmutation of designs and colors, the most reliable way to identify a pile rug's origin is through a close examination of the texture created on the back by the rows of knots and the wefts that separate them.

The primary clue is the weft: the color and spin of the material used; the thickness and firmness of the ply; the number of wefts; the degree of tension that was exerted as the wefts passed between each row of knots; and the firmness that was used to beat the wefts down against the knots.

The next most important clue is the spin and thickness of the yarn used for knotting and the tightness of the loop around the warps. The type of knot employed can be determined to be symmetrical (Turkish) or asymmetrical (Persian) by "breaking the rug open," that is, folding it back parallel to a line of wefting. If the fully revealed knots cover two warp threads with the yarn ends emerging between them, the knot is symmetrical. If only one of the warps is visible between the emerging yarn, it is asymmetrical. (For more detailed information, see the section on pile knots in chapter 2). Finally, depending on the degree of depression or displacement of alternate warp threads, the surface of the back may be flat or slightly to markedly ribbed.

All of the previous clues are the result of weaving techniques absorbed by children seated at looms alongside female relatives manipulating yarns in a linked series of rapid actions as unthinking as breathing. Once learned, these techniques are strongly resistant to change, except in the rare case of an independent-minded weaver with a yen for experimentation.

Other elements contributing to accurate identification are the dye colors, the finished rug's relative firmness or floppiness, the length and luster of the wool, and, assuming they are original, the edge binding and end finish.

Assigning an ambiguous weave to a specific place and time causes heated controversy among scholars and collectors, because in all forms of collecting, provenance—which confirms that the object collected is what it is claimed to be—is extremely important. Since weavers rarely kept records of their work, subjective opinions about rug provenance based on lists of dyestuffs in old bills of lading and imperfectly translated journals by travelers of dubious reliability are rampant. Thanks to the addition of oriental rug studies to college-level arts programs, this unhappy situation is rapidly changing for the better, and the large number of authoritative books and journals now available give novice collectors a much better chance of making accurate identifications.

Fakes

Dealers' prices and auction estimates are based primarily on a rug's age, condition, and rarity. Compared to other collecting fields, rug fakery is uncommon, but a mellow antique look can be counterfeited with skillfully applied chemical washes, and the polished look of a rug's back smoothed of wool fuzz through years of use can be achieved in minutes with a blowtorch.

A rug in mint condition purported to be antique demands confirmation as such by a qualified expert. Some of the classical carpets hotly competed for by wealthy collectors before the 1929 crash were later revealed as counterfeit. Ten years ago, at the height of a collecting craze for soumak bags, new bags expertly woven with old materials brought high prices at auction houses. Today, badly worn antique Caucasian rugs are being completely "restored" by removing the worn pile from the foundation and reknotting the pattern with old wool unraveled from flat weaves. Most of this work is being done in Turkey, and the refurbishment is so good that some experienced dealers and auction house experts have been fooled. Daniel Shaffer, the editor of *HALI,* says that given a few years of use, these fakes may be impossible to tell from the real thing. The beginning collector of Caucasians should be alert to (1) a substantial use of yellow, which is a popular color with buyers and (2) the absence of dirt compacted around the base of the knots.

Contemporary copies of antique Turkish rugs are also sometimes claimed to be the real thing. Be suspicious of fringes lacking signs of age and wear, wool pile evenly clipped to emulate the effect of corroded black and brown naturally dyed wool, and the overall muted tonality characteristic of a chemical wash. The best of these copies are well worth buying (for a discussion of contemporary collectibles, see chapter 10), but not for the price of genuine antique.

Condition

Leaving aside the special instances mentioned earlier, a rug's condition can easily be determined simply by taking the time to see if it exhibits any of the following problems. But first, be aware that pile worn evenly low will affect value less than uneven wear. It may even enhance the clarity of the design of finely knotted pieces.

If a rug was reduced in size to fit a particular space or to eliminate damaged portions, it should be priced accordingly. If done well, reductions can easily elude detection. Look for missing borders and oddly proportioned field patterns.

Other value-affecting problems include:

1. Rebound or new selvages, especially if the wefts were cut

2. Damaged or missing fringes or plain-woven skirts

3. Cotton fringes added to wool-warped rugs

4. Wear creases

5. Insect damage

6. Holes

7. Stains

8. Unsightly repairs

9. Bleeding, faded, or strident dyes

10. Paint used to disguise a worn foundation, conceal bleeding dyes, or brighten faded colors

11. Dry rot (cotton foundations only)

12. Glued-on backing or reinforcement tape

13. Ripples caused by uneven tension

14. Skewed dimensions (tolerated in tribal rugs if moderate)

Before making a final judgment about an appealing rug with any of these problems, review your primary reason for wanting it. There is much less need for a decorative furnishing rug to retain its structural integrity than a collectible piece. A carpet intended for a dining room will benefit from sturdily rebound edges, and if its borders are wonderful, a worn section in the central field—which will be hidden under the table—can be used as a bargaining chip.

The last step? Unless the location of the showroom makes it impossible, ask to see the rug in daylight. Artificial light enhances the beauty of pile made with lustrous wool, but daylight is best for judging the quality of the color and detection of dye runs.

Dealers Versus Auctions

If dealers in collectible rugs acquire a good piece relatively cheaply, they may either pass on part of their savings to a loyal customer or mark it at the going price to cushion losses on rugs they may be unable to sell for enough to cover their cost. Pricing also depends on how easily a rug can be replaced by one of similar age and quality, and whether it is currently hot or has passed its peak of popularity.

An auction provides a public marketplace where rugs must sell within minutes of their introduction from the podium. Since a handling fee is charged for unsold rugs, it is in the consignor's interest to accept a realistic range of estimates. In order to protect the consignor's original cost, most rugs will also have a cut-off or "reserve" price—known only to the auction house—that bids must meet or exceed before they can be sold.

Auction attendees intending to bid are required to register before being assigned numbers. In New York State, auctioneers are legally required to state publicly the failure of a lot to sell. Elsewhere, rugs are commonly "knocked down" to numbers an auction house assigns to itself, so when lots that fail to meet the low estimate are consistently awarded to the same two or three numbers, it can be assumed they failed to meet the reserve price. If, however, a winning bid zooms well above the high estimate, it can indicate one of three things: (1) the auction house experts undervalued the merits of the rug, (2) a dealer or decorator has a well-heeled client who expressed interest in it, or (3) the buyer, either driven by ego or out of ignorance, was willing to pay an inflated price to get it.

Auctions can be both entertaining and instructive, but since no returns or exchanges are permitted, buying at auction is best suited to cool-headed types able to stick to a predetermined bidding limit. Many experienced collectors prefer the flexibility inherent in buying from dealers sensitive to their particular requirements. This said, please keep in mind the difference between a rug dealer's stock and that of dealers in other forms of art. Since rugs appeal to both the tactile and visual senses, collectors would, ideally, like to see and feel every rug on offer. But large carpets are heavy and awkward to roll out and up again, and displaying all the scatter or area rugs stacked in piles is a labor-intensive process. Collectors more interested in indulging their passion for looking at rugs than buying one can soon reduce a shop to shambles. Auctions can never replace the special relationship many "ruggies" have with dealers, but the sale previews allow them to look and touch to their collecting hearts' content. ◘

2

HOW ORIENTAL RUGS ARE MADE

The definition of handmade rugs provided by A. F. Kendrick and C. E. C. Tattersall in *Hand-Woven Carpets*, published in 1922, has yet to be improved on in terms of visual clarity:

The whole field of hand-made carpets can be divided into two great classes—those with smooth faces and those with a pile. Both . . . are textile fabrics, which means they consist essentially of two sets of threads—the warp and the weft—which cross each other at right angles and are interwoven so as to make a coherent tissue. The smooth-faced carpets consist of warp and weft alone; the pile carpets have, in addition, short extra pieces of thread knotted to the warp threads so that their free ends stand up and form a surface similar to blades of grass in a meadow.

Rug-Making Materials

The principal fibers used in rug making are sheep's wool, silk, camel hair, and goat hair. The earliest rugs were either felted or coarsely knotted of thick, long-piled wool for the purpose of insulating against the cold. Sheep's wool is the most commonly used material; camel and goat hair is found primarily in tribal nomadic weavings. Goat hair is generally too stiff to be used for knotting, but it is frequently incorporated into woolen warp yarns to provide extra strength, and tribal weavers often employ it to reinforce edge finishes.

Hand-spun wool yarns were commonly used for both warps and wefts in cottage and tribal weavings, and in many cases still are, but improvements in transportation have made cotton available to weavers in heretofore remote areas. Virtually all twentieth-century village and urban workshop carpets have mill-spun cotton foundations. Cotton is stable and strong, and although it is subject to dry rot in humid environments, cotton foundations lie flatter than those made of wool. For this reason, cotton was the fiber of choice for both warps and wefts in antique Persian and Chinese carpets and in the wefts of some late nineteenth-century Caucasian rugs. The presence of cotton in a rug foundation provides an important clue to both the date and place of its manufacture.

Silk has been used through the centuries for both the pile and foundations of very fine carpets, and is sometimes knotted into wool pile to provide lustrous accents. Shiny mercerized cotton, which is used for both the foundation and pile of cheap souvenir mats touted as "art silk," is occasionally seen as an accent in tribal weavings.

Before a fiber can be spun into yarn, the shorn wool or hair must be cleaned of twigs, seeds, and burrs. Sheep fleeces are usually washed after shearing, but

Rug-Making Materials— Spinning. Turkish woman spinning with drop spindle. Photo courtesy of Gayle Garrett.

the wonderfully lustrous pile in some tribal weaving leads one to suspect that this step may be omitted. After washing, wool is sorted to separate light from dark fibers before being combed to remove the short fibers. The remaining long fibers are first arranged so that they lie parallel to one another, then they are spun into a strong, smooth-surface yarn.

Spinning is usually considered women's work, but in some areas it is also an acceptable task for men. In rug-weaving cultures, people spin while tending their flocks, walking to and from fields and orchards, and tending babies or waiting for a pot to boil. In short, they spin whenever two hands are not needed for the task at hand. A simple device known as a spindle is used for this purpose, and some of its many forms predate the wheel.

The initial thread is spun by twisting fibers into a continuous strand, after which a small spinning wheel–like device is used to twist several strands together in the opposite direction of the original spin to form the yarn. The tightness and number of combined threads determine a yarn's thickness and use. Two to four firmly plied stout strands are used for the warps, weft yarns are thinner and less strongly plied, and the yarn used for the pile is even more loosely combined to ensure a smooth lustrous surface.

Rug Dyes

If you ask a rug aficionado to name the three most important elements a collectible carpet should have, the inevitable answer is, "Color, color, and color." And, inevitably, you will be told that the color must have been obtained from vegetable or insect-derived dyes.

Although it is possible to duplicate synthetically the most subtle shades of natural colors, when synthetic dyes were first seen by weavers in remote areas, they were admired for their uncompromising brightness, and since the drawbacks were as yet unknown, they were happily used to dye the silk knotted in for highlights.

Natural dyes have never been abundantly available, and preparing them properly requires considerable skill, so it is hardly surprising that the use of synthetic dyes, which can be applied with a precision impossible with vegetable dyes, was not only encouraged, but also required by the booming revival of the carpet trade in the late nineteenth century. But unless carpets could be supplied to meet the taste of unsophisticated Western buyers unfamiliar with traditional oriental rug palettes, sizes, and patterns, the revival was sure to be short lived. Most of the early easy-to-use synthetic dyes employed to meet those commercial demands were neither light nor water-fast, and their use in carpets that were otherwise well made became disastrous to the point that they were banned from Turkish and Persian workshops. Unfortunately, cheap synthetic dyes continued to deface cottage rugs until the reintroduction of natural dyes twenty-five years ago.

Synthetic dyes have improved enormously over the years, and today the retail market offers a wide choice of handsome carpets colored with them. Assuming one chooses a well-made piece to begin with, rugs dyed with today's superior synthetics will retain their value. The relationship to an antique rug woven in a traditional context will remain that of a good reproduction, but as time goes by, the ability to make this distinction may become blurred as copies more and more resemble the real thing. The purist, however, will not accept synthetic dyes in a collectible weaving and is offended by synthetics manipulated to ape the imprecision of natural dyes.

All dyes have a chemical makeup, but natural dyes, even when expertly made and applied, yield by their very nature imprecise results that synthetic dyes do not. Natural dyes cannot produce hard-edged colors like the synthetics because the decocted plants and insects contain a myriad of chemical constituents that make it impossible to exactly reproduce a particular hue in succeeding dye lots. Thanks to the naturally occurring chemical overlaps between one color and another, these slight variations are hardly ever disharmonious.

The shimmering pointillist effect of the best antique carpets is not the result of quality control; rather, it is a felicitous, accidental by-product. The shadings of pile color known as abrash occur because of the impossibility of avoiding variation in color from one dye lot to the next when using natural dyestuffs. Vegetable dye colorants are the product not only of a particular plant, but also of the conditions in which it grows: altitude, soil, moisture, and maturity when harvested and the mineral content of the water used for the dye bath. All of these factors are largely a matter of circumstance, including the way in which the dye is absorbed by the yarn used to make a particular rug.

In addition, pile mellowed by sunlight, dust, and smoke during years of respectful domestic use acquires a unique patina and authenticity that to an educated eye and sensibility distinguishes one rug from another no matter how similar they may seem to a layperson.

Part of the appeal of natural dyes is the romance inherent in names that bring to mind Egyptian pyramids, Imperial Rome, Middle Eastern dynasties, and the black tents of nomads. The following is a list of the most commonly encountered natural dyes, along with the metal salts introduced to create a chemical bond between the dyestuff and animal fibers, some of which will not unite with the colorants unaided. Known as mordants, the name comes from the Latin *mordere,* which means "to bite."

Indigo (*Indigofera tinctoria* [true indigo]; *Isatis tinctoria* [woad]), the most commonly used of all dyes, has to undergo a complex process in a fermentation vat because the blue dye obtained from the leaves is not water soluble. The natural and synthetic forms are indistinguishable and both may be obtained from chemical supply houses.

There are a number of ways of incorporating the insoluble blue powder in a solution, but whichever is chosen, the yarn is first dipped in the resulting greenish-yellow liquid then lifted out and exposed to air. After being united with oxygen, the coloring matter deposited on the yarn turns blue, which will deepen with repeated immersions and airings. Indigo-dyed yarn mordanted with the appropriate metal salts can be overdyed with yellow or red to produce greens and purples. Although dependably light- and water-fast, indigo is subject to color loss through abrasion because it is deposited on the yarn rather than absorbed into it.

Madder (*Rubia tinctorum*) grows both wild and under cultivation. It is an ancient dyestuff and its colorfastness ranks very high. The dye resides in the red material beneath the outer bark of roots three years old or more, which are then dried and ground into a powder.

Madder yields a clear red varying in shade from orange-red to garnet to violet, depending on the amount of color-influencing compounds present in the plant and the mineral salts used to mordant the wool. In the Melas area of Turkey, a strong orange is obtained from local wild madder plants.

Exquisite rugs have been woven with wool colored with nothing more than indigo and madder, a selection of mordants, and undyed light and dark wool.

Cochineal (*Dactylopius coccus*) is a red dye obtained from an insect cultivated on cactus plants, principally in Mexico and Central America. About seventy thousand dried insects yield one pound of powdered dyestuff. The Spanish introduced the dye to Europe in the 1500s, but it was not used to any great extent in oriental carpets until the nineteenth century.

Cochineal dyes usually have a cooler tonality than madder, and for a long time the term "crimson" was applied solely to the bluish-red color chiefly associated with it. Another insect-derived dye is lac, which was used in early Persian carpets and extensively in India.

Weld (*Reseda luteola*) is an annual herb that grows about three feet high. It is the best source of yellow and almost as lightfast as indigo and madder. All parts of the plant except the roots can be used, and depending on the mordant, a bright yellow to gold to yellow-green may be obtained.

Oak (*Quercus*, in variety) and tanner's sumach (*Rhus coriaria*) produce black and dark brown dyes when wool mordanted with iron salts is treated with the tannins extracted from these sources. Unfortunately, the effect of the combined iron and tannin is corrosive, and wool treated with it becomes brittle over time. This effect is so well known that black-dyed wool used in copies of old rugs is often clipped to simulate the look of corroded pile.

Mordants used to "fix" dyestuffs to wool and silk fibers can significantly affect color tones. Tin is used to brighten a color, and iron salts to darken or "sadden." Other minerals used are alum, chrome, and carbonate of soda.

Middle Eastern dyers traditionally color the fibers after they have been spun into yarn. If mordants are needed, they will be dissolved and applied first. After drying, the yarn is then immersed in vats of the dyeing solution and allowed to remain for varying amounts of time depending on the shade desired. Succeeding uses of the dye bath will yield paler hues. After dyeing, the wool is rinsed until the water runs clear, as even a fast color will bleed at a later washing if insufficiently rinsed initially. The wool is dried again before collection or purchase by the weaver.

Although natural colors soften after long exposure to light and wear, Western eyes used to the mellow look of well-used antique carpets can be jolted by the brilliance of new vegetable-dyed wool. Rugs shielded for centuries from strong light—a prime example is the extraordinary collection housed in the Black Church in Brasov, Romania—are as bright as when they were newly made.

Synthetic Dyes

The first commercially successful synthetic dye was mauveine, which was accidentally discovered in 1856 by a British chemist as a by-product of the oxidation of aniline, a coal-tar derivative. About ten years later, a group of more brilliant, magenta-toned dyes—generally referred to as fuchsine—supplanted the paler, rapidly fleeting mauve.

The presence of these later aniline dyes in late nineteenth-century rugs can be detected by their absence. Antique rugs with areas of gray or beige in their designs often retain a trace of the original magenta on the back of the foundation. When these early synthetic dyes faded, the coloring substance didn't vanish into thin air. Triggered by light or moisture, a chemical change occurred within the dyestuff, creating a new compound that was colorless, less highly colored, or of a different color altogether. Instead of merely softening, like natural dyes, the tonality often shifted enough to destroy the color balance of the entire rug.

To subdue the strident, hard-edged look of some synthetics, chemical washes were—and still are—routinely used to a lesser or greater degree, depending on the effect desired. The color-mellowing, luster-enhancing result can indeed improve the overall look, but if injudiciously used, these washes can rob wool of its natural lubrication and affect its wearability.

The makeup of modern synthetic dyes is very complex. Not all of them are reliable, but the fastness of the better varieties are good to excellent. The interest of dedicated collectors extends beyond the technical minutiae of rug making to the historic and ethnic context, but a well-made synthetically dyed carpet crafted to look as much like its antique original as today's technical advances allow will provide many years of trouble-free service for anyone interested primarily in a decorative floor furnishing.

The Weaving Process

Textile fabrics, including carpets, are woven on a frame or loom, the complexity of which is determined by the type and size of the article to be woven and the workplace of the weaver. Urban workshops have larger, more elaborate looms than cottage and nomadic weavers, but the essentials remain the same. Nomadic weavers, who must transport their looms from place to place, wind the warp threads over horizontal beams held in place by stakes driven into the ground.

The beams of cottage looms, which are typically constructed from roughly cobbled timber, are secured by sturdy upright side pieces and housed in the family dwelling so that women may weave rugs, either for domestic use or to supplement the family's income, when not engaged in household chores.

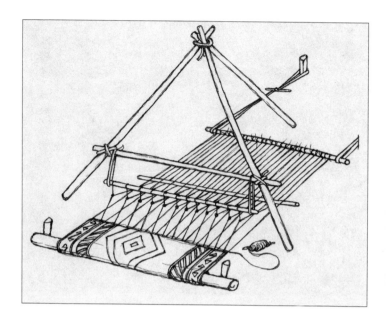

Commercial village and urban looms use roller-beam looms of various degrees of sophistication, in which the upper and lower beams rotate, allowing the completed portion of the rug to be wound around the lower beam while additional warp is unwound from the upper, making it possible to weave rugs of any desired length.

The Weaving Process. A nomadic ground loom.

Portable ground looms accommodate one weaver; cottage looms allow two or three weavers to sit side by side, the better to exchange village gossip as their fingers fly between the warps. The width of urban looms can be adjusted to accommodate the demands of the international market, and the number of weavers required is determined accordingly.

Warp threads, which are subject to greater stress than the wefts that cross them, are generally the thicker and stronger of the two. The warps are strung vertically on the beams, and lie parallel to the side pieces and each other. The closeness of the warps, which depends on the thickness of the yarn used, determines the fineness of the weaving to be done. The warps on the two edges are customarily stouter than those in

between and are left free of pile knots so they may be strengthened and securely fastened to the body of the rug with extra turns of the weft threads. After the rug is completed, the edges are reinforced with wool, goat hair, or cotton threads, the choice being a clue to a rug's origin.

Once the warp threads are set in place, the weft threads are woven over and under alternate warps across the width of the vertically strung warp yarn, with each passage of weft reversing the course of the previous one. If you've ever darned a hole in a sock or sweater, you are already familiar with this process and can readily imagine the tedium of applying it to the scale of a large carpet.

Fortunately, weavers long ago figured out how to speed the process by passing a flat stick about two inches wide over and under the warp threads, but above the area where the actual weaving will take place. This stick divides the warp threads into two sets or planes, forming a space called a shed between them, which allows the weft thread to be passed through the divided warps in one smooth thrust.

For the alternate passage of the weft, the position of the rear set of warps must be exchanged for the set in front. To accomplish this, all of the warp threads at the rear of the shed are attached with short equal cords to a rod. When this rod is drawn forward, the attached warps are pulled to the front, creating a space through which the next "shoot" of weft is passed. This exchange of one set of warps with the other is repeated throughout the weaving process.

NOTE: If, like many beginning collectors, you have trouble visualizing the process of weaving a three-dimensional object from a written explanation or a two-dimensional diagram, you may find it well worth your time to build and rig a simple tabletop loom. Instructions can be found in G. W. Scott's *An Illustrated Guide to Making Oriental Rugs.*

Knotted Pile Rugs

If a weaver intends to make a pile rug, a simple interweaving of the weft with the warp is usually done at the bottom of the rug where it begins, and again at the top after the pile knotting is completed. Another clue to a rug's origin is provided by the way in which these plain-woven ends terminate. The warps may be left hanging loose in a simple fringe, knotted, or braided into a coarse netting. In some weaving areas, a narrow band of plain weave is simply turned under and sewn to the back of the rug. Old Turkoman carpets may have red skirts up to ten inches wide, narrowly striped in blue or otherwise decorated, and the woven ends in the best Baluch tribal work are elaborately patterned. Whatever the end finish, when repairs are needed, the weaver's original choice should be respected.

When the initial band of plain weave is completed, a first row of knots is tied to the warps, followed by one or more weft yarns. If two wefts are used between each row of knots, the thread is taken through the shed from one side of the loom to the other in a single shoot, and is immediately returned through the reversed shed space. If only one weft is inserted, a technique characteristic of the Hamadan district of Iran, then the reversed-shed weft isn't returned until after the completion of a row of knots. Antique Kazak rugs from the south Caucasus may have three or four red-dyed wefts clearly visible between each row of knots. In others, like nineteenth-century Persian Kermans and Bidjars, one or more of the wefts are hidden from sight within the structure. In other words, the color, placement, and number of wefts "laid in" between each row of knots is as distinctive as a bit of DNA.

The knots used to secure wool yarn to warp threads are not tied knots in the same sense as those used to secure boats to docks or hooks to fishing line. Pile knots, made by looping a length of yarn around warp threads, are held in place by the pressure exerted both by the adjacent knots and the next passage of weft or wefts pressed down very hard against them with a comb-like tool known as a beater.

Weavers commonly use their fingers to tie the yarn, which is then cut with a knife snugged into the palm. In some Iranian districts, a tool known as a *tikh*, whose knife has a hooked end, is used both to pull the pile yarn around the warps and to cut it after the knot is completed. Whichever method is employed, it is always a loop-and-cut process. Oriental rug weavers never use short precut pieces of wool for the pile.

The two knots most commonly used for the pile in oriental rugs are the Persian, an asymmetrical knot referred to in older rug publications as Senneh (or Sehna), after a Persian district, and the Turkish, a symmetrical knot formerly identified as Ghiordes, a famed Turkish weaving center. The confusion generated by the use of geographical labels for an element of rug structure that disregards national boundaries has led to an almost universal substitution of the terms "asymmetrical" (asym) for the Persian knot and "symmetrical" (sym) for the Turkish knot in rug books and auction catalogs.

Turkish knots are used in Turkey/Anatolia and the Caucasus, both Persian and Turkish knots are used in Iran/Persia, and the Persian knot is also found in In-

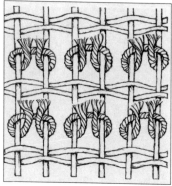

dian, Chinese, and most Turkoman rugs. Although some antique Turkoman rugs have Turkish knots along the edges, the Persian knot is generally used elsewhere. Some authorities maintain that the Persian knot is more suited to finely detailed curvilinear patterns than the Turkish, but the choice of knot is dictated by tradition rather than any advantage one may have over the other.

Both types of knots occupy adjacent warps. Symmetrically knotted yarn lies across and on top of the paired warps with the free ends emerging between them. Two little bumps or nodes on the back of a rug identify a knot as symmetrical, but since the space occupied by these two nodes is broader than it is high, there are fewer knots per inch horizontally than vertically.

One end of an asymmetrically knotted yarn completely surrounds one warp; the other passes behind the second warp and emerges outside of it, but the encircled warp thread may be either the right or left thread of the pair. Asymmetrical knots opening to the left incline the pile to the right; those opening to the right, incline it to the left.

In some asymmetrically knotted rugs, the tension of the wefts crossing between the knots is deliberately varied so as to strongly displace one of the paired warps, thus pulling the emerging pile yarns closer together. Since this is hard to visualize from a written description, try holding up two fingers to represent a pair of warps, with the knuckles becoming the two nodes of a single knot. If you keep your fingers in the same plane, both knuckle-nodes are clearly visible, but by inclining your fingers from the horizontal to the vertical planes, you can see one of the nodes becoming less and less visible, as if depressed by the pressure of a tightly drawn weft.

When one of the paired warps is displaced, the back of the rug displays nodes that no longer lie parallel to one another. Instead, you will see a small square created by one node rather than the rectangle typical of two. This allows the overall horizontal knot count to equal that of the vertical, thereby minimizing the distortion of complex designs copied from an artist's drawing known as a cartoon.

All of these elements—the set of the warps, the fineness of weft, the type of knot, and the fiber and sizes of yarn used—determine the amount of design detail the weaver is able to translate into pile, the completed rug's "handle"—stiff, supple, meaty, or flabby—and its resistance to wear over time.

A highly skilled weaver can tie up to a thousand knots an hour. As a general rule, very finely knotted rugs are more expensive than those of average knot count, but to connoisseurs, knot density is irrelevant. The breath-robbing impact of the best examples of tribal weaving can make collectors eager to part with large sums of money for small works of coarsely knotted textile art.

Rugs may be woven by a single nomadic tribeswoman knotting traditional patterns from memory or, at the other extreme, in a shop filled with looms on which identical carpets are woven in sections by teams of weavers following the knot sequence called out in a rhythmic drone. The number of knots per square inch can vary from about sixteen to a thousand. In a few museum-quality Mughal prayer rugs, the count reaches an incredible two thousand. Most carpets have between fifty and one hundred knots; some boast three hundred or more, but little is gained by a knot count exceeding four hundred.

Is there an ideal carpet structure? That depends entirely on the use to which it will be put. A finely knotted silk prayer rug appropriate for an elegant bedroom or draped across a Steinway, would look fussy in a converted rural barn, which would be better served by a boldly patterned, coarsely knotted Turkish cottage rug. Generally speaking, however, rugs well made of good materials and of average coarseness are more satisfactory as floor furnishings than finely knotted ones.

When a completed rug is removed from the loom, the cut warps may be left as a fringe or knotted into slender bundles or netting to protect the pile knots from erosion. The pile, which was only roughly cut during the weaving, is then given a final clipping, either by the weaver or, in the case of urban workshops, a precise shearing by a master craftsman. The lush pastel floral designs of some modern commercially designed Chinese and Indian carpets are usually embossed by clipping a groove around the principal motifs, thus creating an opulent three-dimensional look.

The final step in the finishing process is a thorough washing, ranging from soap and water to a further treatment with chemicals to soften colors considered too strident and heighten the pile's natural luster. Collectors will accept a mild chemical wash in a furnishing rug, but in a collectible rug, any hint of past chemical manipulation of the dyes or pile will affect its desirability.

Flat-Woven Rugs

Some flat weaves are very finely woven and intricately patterned—the wonderful Persian Senneh kilims are a prime example. Some combine more than one technique in a single piece. But the plain-woven antique kilims incorporating bold motifs with bands and blocks of vibrant color are the most sought after by specialist collectors, who consider pile rugs fussy and insipid in comparison.

 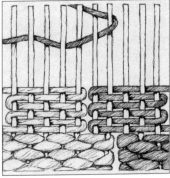

Plain Weave.
Plain weave
structure.

Kilim. Tapestry
weave used in
kilims.

Rug scholars differ widely on how best to group and describe flat-weave techniques. Novice collectors are understandably bewildered by this large, complex class of weavings, but all flat-woven, smooth-faced textiles, to quote again Kendrick and Tattersall in *Hand-Woven Carpets*, "consist essentially of two sets of threads which cross each other at right angles and are interwoven."

Plain Weave
The alternate interlacing of warp and weft produces a simple, balanced, plain-woven textile. If, however, either the warp or weft dominates—that is, if one set of threads is more visible than the other—the result is known as a warp- or weft-faced weave.

Kilim
The weft-faced plain weave known as tapestry weave is used for kilims, in which the warps are entirely concealed by beaten-down colored wefts woven in blocks rather than continuously across the loom. These discontinuous wefts turning back into their own color blocks create a slit between the warps of one block and the adjoining block of another color.

Sometimes this slit is left open to serve as part of the design. Sometimes it is eliminated by dovetailing the wefts of adjacent blocks on a single warp, or it may be sewn shut after the weaving is completed. Occasionally, the slit is closed by a supplementary weft in a contrasting color or sheathed in gold or silver, thus adding glitter to the overall pattern.

Because they are the most easily woven, geometric patterns are the norm for flat-weave textiles, but curvilinear designs can be created by beating down the wefts tightly in some areas and looser in others. This demanding technique, known as eccentric wefting, was used in some early Ottoman Turkish kilims and in the contemporary Turkish copies of elegant floral kilims made in the Balkans.

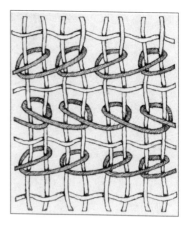

Soumak. The soumak weave with shoots of weft alternating with warp-wrapping wefts.

Soumak

In soumaks, the wefts wrap entirely around the warps. When these wefts alternate with shoots of simple interwoven wefts, the wrapping wefts are considered supplementary rather than an integral part of the structure.

Warp-wrapping sequences, which are dictated by tradition, vary from district to district and provide the expert eye with an important clue to a soumak's origin.

Brocade, Weft Float, and Embroidery

This may be a good time to take a deep breath. The term "brocade" as applied to flat-woven textiles refers to the addition of discontinuous supplementary warps or wefts to a basic plain woven structure.

If, however, continuous wefts are used to create a surface pattern, they are temporarily discontinued or "floated" on the back of the textile between pattern areas.

Brocading and weft-float techniques are used during the weaving process and are part of the structure. Decoration added with a needle after the textile is taken off the loom is considered to be embroidered.

Glossary of Basic Rug-Weaving Terms

Abrash—Variations in the coloration of bands of rug pile resulting from the subtle differences from one dye bath to another when the dyestuff is obtained from natural sources.

Aniline—the name given to early synthetic dyes that tended to bleed when washed and fade over time to gray or beige.

Beaten up, down, or in—refers to wefts being forced down against a preceding row of knots with a large, multitined wooden or metal tool.

Carding—the process of cleaning and intermixing fibers with carders, a pair of combs with bent and angled wire teeth.

Cartoon—a drawing showing a section of rug design usually made to order by artists. They can also be bought ready-made by village weavers and varied as desired.

Combing—preparing wool for spinning by combing out the short fibers and arranging the remaining long fibers in parallel order.

Dovetailing—a flat-weave technique in which wefts from adjacent color areas share a common warp so as to eliminate the slit associated with tapestry weaving.

Fibers Used in Rug Making

Cotton—a cellulose vegetable fiber with a flattened tubular structure. Although stronger wet than dry, moisture affects its elasticity and if prolonged promotes dry rot.

Silk—a protein fiber much finer than those from other animal sources. A silk filament from 499 to 1,000 yards can be obtained from a single silkworm cocoon.

Sheep's wool, camel hair, and goat hair—these fibers have an infinite number of small scales that allow them to bend without breaking. The quality of the fiber depends on the animal's breeding, age, pasturage, from what part of the animal the wool or hair was taken, and whether the animal was alive or dead. Animal fibers are stronger dry than wet. They are vulnerable to insect damage, but are not subject to dry rot.

Other Terms Used in Rug Making

Flat weave—a textile created by the interweaving of horizontal wefts with vertical warps in any one of several interlocking techniques.

Handle—this describes the weight and flexibility of a rug.

Heddle—the rods to which alternate warps are attached so they may drawn forward and backward to create a space for facilitating the passage of weft threads from one side of the loom to the other.

Knots—the knots most commonly used to loop pile yarn around warps are the asymmetrical Persian or Senneh (Sehna) knot and the symmetrical Turkish or Ghiordes knot.

kpsi—abbreviation used in rug descriptions for knots per square inch.

Pick—the passage of one thread of weft through the warps, also known as a shoot. This passage of wefts is sometimes described as being "laid in the shed."

Selvage or **selvedge**—made by the encirclement of wefts around the bundles of warps at a rug's vertical edges and often reinforced by overwrapping with wool yarn or goat hair.

Shed—the space formed when warps are separated into two planes by a long flat stick threaded in between and then turned on edge. This space, which is more efficiently created with a heddle, allows the swift passage of a shuttle carrying the wefts from one side to the other.

Shuttle—a device around which a weft thread is wound to prevent it from tangling and to ease its passage though the shed.

Spindle—a simple handheld tool resembling an elongated toy top with which clumps of carded wool hooked or slotted onto it are transformed into yarn as it drops while spinning.

Warp—the strong foundation yarn threaded from top to bottom on a loom and interwoven with thinner wefts.

Weft—the thread or yarn interwoven with the strung warps. Wefts separate and anchor the rows of knots in pile rugs. In flat-woven textiles, wefts may be continuous, as they are in pile rugs, or discontinuous, supplementary, or floated, depending on the desired effect.

Wool yarns—oriental rug yarns are worsted-spun from wool's long, lustrous fibers that with wear acquire a characteristic paintbrush-like tip. Worsted yarns are also used for fine suiting fabrics. The fluffy yarns typical of short fibers are unable to resist the stress of the weaving process.

Yarn ply and twist—the twist of the threads spun into yarn is described either as "Z" or "S," depending on the direction of the spun yarn's slant. The initial spun thread is a single. Singles combine into one ply. Two singles twisted together are two ply; three singles, three ply, and so on. When yarn singles are plied together, the twist is invariably opposite that of the initial thread's twist. In structural analyses provided in books and auction catalogs, the notation "Z2S" stands for a yarn made up of two single Z-spun strands S-plied together.

For more detailed information, consult the annotated list of books, periodicals, and websites in the Resource Guide. ◙

3

RUG FORMATS

Since creativity has little place in cultures that consider innovation a threat to traditional custom and values, the rugs treasured by Western collectors invariably prove to be inspired variations on time-honored themes.

Once it is accepted that the term "unique" can rarely be applied to an oriental rug, the collector looks for excellence in the following three areas:

1. The choice, clarity, and use of colors derived from natural dyes

2. The relationship between the size of the rug, the design elements within it—field, borders, spandrels, and medallions—and of those elements to each other

3. The selection and spacing of incidental motifs

Up until the last quarter of the nineteenth century, the sizes of oriental weavings were dictated by traditional room sizes and domestic needs. Weavers using ground looms or the simplest of vertical types made pile and flat-weave textiles in a variety of shapes and sizes for domestic storage, the transport of goods and crops, and horse and camel trappings, sometimes gaily decorated for the use at weddings and the like.

In traditional Persian homes, four narrow rugs—marketed today as "long" or "corridor" rugs—were arranged in a long rectangle. One was placed sideways at the top, while the other three were placed side by side beneath it, an arrangement allowing for considerable flexibility.

The length of the museum-worthy carpets made for wealthy patrons were generally two to three times their width. The sizes of smaller rugs made for domestic use by cottage and village weavers are usually found to have a proportion of roughly one and a half feet in length for every foot in width.

The artistry inherent in a fine rug can only be fully appreciated if it can be placed in a room so that it can be seen in its entirety. Unfortunately, Westerners tend to choose rugs in sizes that all but blanket the floor space of a given room, and then obscure its admirably proportioned design elements with furniture.

Terminology

Each rug-weaving district has its own name for every size, shape, and type of woven article, no matter how alike its purpose may be from one place to another. Simplicity is further confounded when these local terms are translated into English, French, German, Italian, and Russian by the authors of books written about them.

In the interest of clarity, the following descriptions of woven textiles will mostly rely on prosaic, use-specific terms. Once you choose an area of concentration, a more sophisticated vocabulary can be acquired via rug literature (consult the lists in the Resource Guide) and from specialist dealers and other collectors.

Rug Sizes

The following sizes of rug categories are given in feet only. Bear in mind, however, that foreign dealers and publications employ the metric system and that in any case antique rugs vary more often than not from these arbitrary dimensions.

Mat

A small rug, roughly 2 × 3 feet, that is used for bedside, doorway, and fireside accents. If there are plain-woven tabs along one side and a skirt along the other, this indicates that the mat was the face of a bag originally used for storage or transport.

Scatter

Scatters range from 2 × 4 to 4 × 6 in varying proportions. Antique rugs in this category were woven by women individually, with friends, or with other family members on cottage looms. Their exuberant coloration and original use of traditional motifs have long recommended them to collectors.

Area Rug/Dozar

Dozar is the term applied by the trade to rugs approximately $4^{1}/_{2}$ × 7 feet. Zar is a traditional Persian unit of measure; a dozar is two zars. However, zars vary in measure from village to village, sometimes by as much as three inches. This may seem odd by Western standards, but Leslie Stroh, the editor of the trade journal *Rug News*, sums it up amusingly in a way that can be applied to Middle Eastern weaving in general, "If you know that he knows that you know, then you both know, and the definition depends not on some abstract measure but on the reality the buyer and seller are confronting . . . there are dozars that actually measure correctly, and dozars that do not . . . [yet all] come into the marketplace with both parties thinking of them as dozars."

Rugs in this group, from thick-piled, boldly colored, geometrically patterned south Caucasian Kazaks to elegantly detailed Sarouk Ferahans, are small enough to be easily handled and stored, yet large enough to make a stunning design statement.

Long or Corridor

These are the rugs made for the traditional arrangement of one over three. They range in size from 5 to 6 × 10 to 12 feet, 6 to 8 × 16 to 20 feet, and 3 to 4 feet × 16 to 20 feet.

Runner

The narrowest long rugs can be used as runners, but a rug designed to be used for that purpose is more likely to have an evenly spaced series of centrally placed motifs. If you plan to use one as a stair carpet, you will be less likely to come to grief on a short-piled, tightly woven rug than one that is glossy, long piled, and loosely woven.

Carpet

A rug ranging from 8 × 10 feet and the more traditional 9 × 11 feet up to 14 × 24 feet is usually referred to as a carpet. Those larger than this are known in the trade as palace carpets.

Prayer

The arch-shaped element at the upper end—occasionally both ends—of a prayer rug symbolizes the mihrab set in the wall of a mosque facing east toward the holy city of Mecca. Although rugs with this format have been commercially popular for centuries, few have actually been used for prayer. Devout Muslims, who are required to use "a clean spot facing Mecca" for the prayers they observe five times daily, often carry a length of sacking or toweling for that worthy purpose.

Made mostly in scatter sizes, prayer rugs have been and still are woven in a wide variety of designs and materials, including the very finely knotted silks intended as wall hangings.

Design Formats
Medallion

This classic rug and carpet format features a medallion or medallions centered in a bordered field or ground. The field may be undecorated or patterned with vines, leaves, flowers, and trees in graceful curvilinear swirls. The floral motifs on rugs woven on cottage looms are usually simpler and more geometric. Tribal weavers often reduce them to symbolic abstractions.

Allover Patterning

If the medallion is removed from a rug's field, what had been a background design can be expanded into a latticed or regimented arrangement that often appears to continue under and beyond the border containing it.

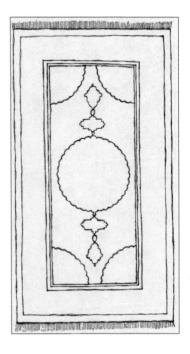

Design Formats— Medallion. Formal medallion rug format.

Compartment

The field is divided into a grid, each cell of which contains repeated motifs, which are often varied as to color and placement to enliven what otherwise might be a static appearance.

Repeats

As typified by Turkoman tribal rugs and carpets, motifs are repeated row after row with little or no variation, but stunning effects are achieved by contrasting the colors chosen for the motifs in succeeding rows or in a stepped color patterning that affects the entire field.

The larger of the two principal motifs seen on Turkoman weavings are known as *guls* and are more generously spaced in antique rugs than on newer examples.

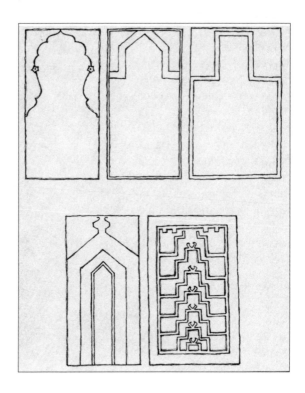

Generally speaking, the newer the carpet with any type of repeat pattern, the more cramped the relationship between the motifs will be.

Pictorial
The woven depiction of famous persons, historical scenes, or traditional legends are often rendered in astonishing detail, but rarely offer much in the way of artistic merit to Western eyes.

Prayer
Below the arch is a space, the mihrab, sometimes open and flanked with one or more pillars, and sometimes decorated with objects symbolizing religious observance, like water pitchers, incense burners, lanterns, or a tree-of-life design. The Metropolitan Museum of Art in New York City has in its collection a particularly fine example of a coupled-column prayer rug created by Ottoman court weavers.

A type of prayer rug known as a *saph* has multiple niches set side by side. Sometimes referred to as family prayer rugs, most authorities agree this format was developed for use in mosques.

Peculiar to Turkey is a prayer rug that contains a series of stepped arches. Versions of this format may be seen in both pile and flat weave.

Sampler

These interesting pieces contain examples of popular field and border motifs knotted in no particular order and are another way designs can be passed from one weaving group to another. Known as *vagireh*, they range in size from mats, to scatters, to occasionally area rug size. They are mainly associated with the Persian Bidjar weaving area and are very popular with collectors.

Dated Rugs

City workshop carpets often have Arabic numerals dating their completion woven into an oblong border element known as a cartouche. Rustic rugs sometimes have dates knotted into the top of the field. In all cases, dates should be regarded with a degree of skepticism:

1. If the shape of the figures eludes easy translation, a dealer aware of how much collectors value age will be tempted to offer as early a dating as can possibly be justified

2. Illiterate weavers sometimes imperfectly knot in dates as a decorative motif

3. Reknotting can transform a late date into an earlier, more desirable one

Flat-Weave Formats
Kilims

The majority of Persian kilims are woven in one piece, are reversible, and are usually of medium size. The exquisite antique Senneh (Sehna) kilims made by Kurdish weavers are much finer and more intricately patterned than the bold geometric norm, and their relatively small size as well as frequent use of a prayer

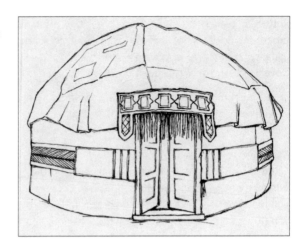

Tent and Yurt Trappings. Yurt with decorative woven door surround.

format make them ideal candidates for wall hangings. Antique examples of flat-woven runners are a sought-after rarity.

With the exception of the beautiful floral kilims made for the Ottoman court, which are rarely available on the market except as fragments, Turkish kilims are usually woven in two matching strips and joined after removal from the loom. Except for those woven in a prayer format, they tend to be much longer than their Persian counterparts. Because of their length, one-half of a Turkish kilim is often used as a runner.

A narrow, tightly interlocked Yomud tribal weaving with geometric motifs arrayed in compressed red, ivory, and dark blue bands is characteristic of the relatively few antique Turkoman kilims seen in the marketplace. More frequently seen are the medium-size reversible Caucasian kilims notable for the size and brilliant coloration of their icon-bearing bands.

The tapestry-woven rugs made in India through the centuries are known as *dhurries*. The large majority of them have been—and still are—made entirely of cotton and are often dismissed as cheap and lacking in durability. But the best antique examples, especially those woven partly of silk, are prized by specialist collectors.

Soumaks

Wherever made, soumaks are usually of medium size and woven in one piece. The most commonly seen are of Caucasian origin, and unlike the previously discussed kilims, the designs are often derived from much older knotted-pile patterns. Particularly popular with collectors are those attributable to the early Caucasian dragon rugs.

Mixed Technique

Small- and medium-size rugs incorporating every variety and combination of the flat-woven techniques discussed earlier have been woven throughout Persia and Turkey, most notably the elegant dark-hued rugs characteristic of Baluch tribal weavers and some large Turkoman rugs, whose plain-weave red grounds are closely covered with weft-float brocade repeats.

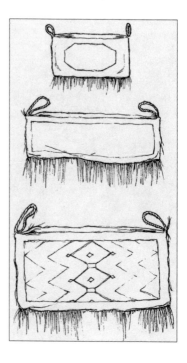

Tent and Yurt Trappings. Three sizes of bags hung from tent and yurt frameworks: 1' x 2'; 1½' x 3'; 3' x 4½'.

Tent and Yurt Trappings

The tents used by Middle Eastern tribal peoples are large sprawling affairs woven from dark brown or black goat hair. Tribes in northern Iran and throughout Central Asia prefer yurts, which is another type of portable structure consisting of a round, domed framework covered with large light-colored felts secured with very long foot-wide, flat-woven bands. These bands are often decorated with pile-knotted animal figures and tribal motifs.

The handsome pile door rugs (*ensi*) hung at the entrance of Turkoman dwellings used to be mistaken for prayer rugs because of the arch-like format. Fixed above the entrance was a three-sided, sometimes tasseled, pile weaving. Antique door surrounds (*kapunuk*) are uncommon in the market and command

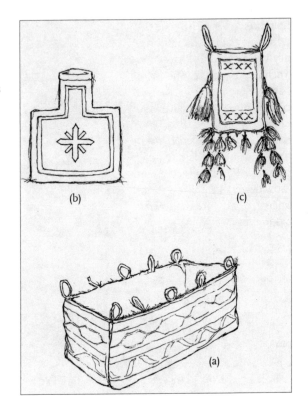

high prices even when the condition leaves some-
thing to be desired.

A narrow flat-woven dining cloth known as a *sofre* is
expressly made and used for the service of food.
Sofres may have mixed-technique borders, but the
center is usually left undyed and undecorated. Oven
cloths (*rukorsi*) are used as the primary cover for the
low table under which a basin of glowing coals is slid
to warm the family sitting around it. The table is covered first with an old blanket, then topped with a
smaller oven cloth displaying a mixed-technique
decoration.

Portable houses require easily transportable furnishings, a need admirably supplied with the wide variety
of flat-woven and pile bags developed for tribal household use. The bags made to store bedding and house-

hold articles or stuffed to use as seats and pillows are generally wider than they are deep. Their faces, which may be pile, flat woven, or a combination of both techniques, are often small works of textile art; the plain-weave backs may repeat in alternating bands the colors seen on the front. Flat-woven tabs projecting along the top edge allow the bags to be hung from the tent or yurt framework at convenient intervals.

Bags intended for the specific purpose of storing grains for human or animal consumption have braided wool or goat hair loops spaced closely along the top so that the opening may be tightly secured against insects and rodents.

Salt and spoon bags depart from the usual wider-than-deep proportions. Salt bags, which vary from about one to two feet square, have a tall narrow chimney-like extension

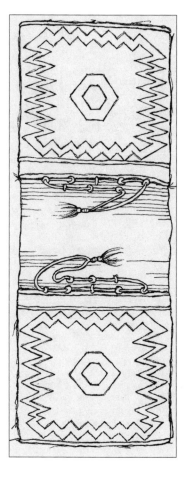

Tent and Yurt Trappings. Saddle bags.

that doubles as a spout and, when flapped over, a closure. The narrow bags used for storing spoons and spindles are attached to the weaver's tent or yurt frame with loops extending from each top corner.

Four-sided storage containers were made by girls of marriageable age to contain the articles woven for their dowries. Given the rarity of complete examples, collectors happily settle for one of the exceptionally well-woven sides.

Another bag format seen throughout the Middle East consists of two smallish bags joined by a flat-woven band. If intended to be carried on an arm, the band will be narrower than one intended to be slung across the back of a horse or donkey. In addition to bags intended to store and transport household goods and foodstuffs or provide seating, a variety of small, often fancifully decorated bags have been woven to contain personal items such as combs, money, and tobacco.

Decorative Animal Trappings

Collections of articles woven and used in a tribal environment invariably include a selection of the wonderful belled, tasseled, and shell-adorned trappings for the heads, chests, flanks, rumps, and even the knees of camels and horses. Some are pile, some flat woven, and some a combination of techniques.

Horse covers are usually flat woven. The size varies from place to place, but the format tends to be similar. Caucasian horse covers (*shadda*) with rows of stylized animals, sometimes in colorful procession, are particularly prized. Saddle covers may be pile or flat woven and the shape varies according to the custom of the weaver's tribe. The most desirable of all are the splendid five-sided—rarely heptagonal—*asmalyks,* which decorate the right and left flanks of a camel carrying a Turkoman bride. ◾

4

RUG MOTIFS

According to the conventional view developed over the years by scholars and collectors, oriental rug designs arose from two different artistic traditions:

1. The curvilinear flower-based designs favored by fifteenth-century Persian court artists and translated by skilled weavers in the palace workshops into finely knotted carpets. A. Cecil Edwards, the author of *The Persian Carpet*, describes the appearance of these palmettes, rosettes, cloud bands, and vases as "isolated from each other, evenly spaced and invariably interconnected into a pattern by some sort of stalk or trellis."

2. The typically rectilinear compartmented Turkish designs are thought to have been derived from carvings on early indigenous stone buildings. These blocky de-

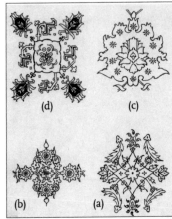

signs are admirably suited to the rather large square knots typical of Turkish weaving. Nomadic weavers tend to favor infinite repeats of geometric designs committed to memory.

The choice and interpretation of motifs is also strongly influenced by the various weaving processes, that is, knotted pile, kilim, soumak, and so on. In the words of the scholar/weaver Marla Mallett, "Design change and disintegration [are] accelerated as motifs migrate from medium to medium, since different technical restraints apply."

Curvilinear Motifs
Boteh
This pear-shaped or curled-leaf design with the bent-over top is found in all types of Persian and Caucasian weavings, but is not part of the Turkish weaving vocabulary. Although primarily seen as a richly colored field motif in horizontal or diagonal rows, the boteh is often used as a filler.

Herati
The sixteenth-century workshops in the city of Herat, which at the time was the principal urban center in eastern Persia, produced beautiful carpets featuring a pattern unit consisting of a blossom within four curv-

ing leaves. At its best when given room to flourish, the Herati became densely packed and distorted in later versions.

Curvilinear Motifs. Boteh variations.

Mina Khani

A favorite of Persian Kurdish weavers, this motif consists of a blossom connected by latticework with four smaller, simpler rosettes. It often appears as a symmetrically placed field design on Veramin and Hamadan rugs, and a version in which the flanking blossoms are knotted in white is seen on some Caucasian Shirvan rugs and on Baluch rugs where the effect of white blossoms on a deep indigo blue or intense madder red is striking. An attractive variation,

consisting of repeated sprays of three white florets, is used as a border motif.

Harshang or Crab

The name "crab" was applied to this irregularly bordered flame-like design by weavers and dealers unfamiliar with its progression from the blossom with leafy projections seen on early rugs made in both Persia and Turkey.

Gol-Farang

Eastern rug weavers responded to the French-influenced fashions popular in Russia in the late nineteenth century with this "foreign flower" motif, composed of flamboyant clusters of roses in full bloom. Realistic roses are found on Persian workshop rugs of the period, while village and tribal weavers produced geometrized versions. These richly colored rugs are best suited to Victorian settings.

Afshan

An open, tulip-shaped flower on a bent stem used as a flanking motif for principal design elements on eighteenth-century Caucasian rugs. A nineteenth-

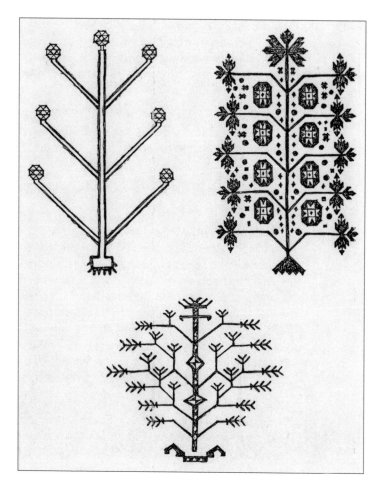

century simplified version seen on Perpedil rugs from
the Kuba area bends the stem at right angles.

**Stylized
Motifs.** Tree-of-
life variations.

Bid Majnun

This appealing "weeping willow" design, a favorite
with Bidjar and other Persian Kurdish village weavers,
combines willows, cypresses, and poplars with vines
and flowers. Derived from early symmetrically format-
ted classic garden rugs, the bid majnun is at its best
when informally arranged.

Tree-of-Life

The universal yearning of humankind for release from
a base, earthly life to the purity of paradise is symbol-

ized by this very old motif seen at its best in simple, sometimes stark versions in tribal and village rugs. When presented realistically in finely knotted workshop carpets, the symbolism tends to be overwhelmed by decoration.

Zil-i-Sultan
A classical Persian flower-and-vase motif either used as a repeat or enlarged to serve as a rug's focal point.

Floral Motifs
A variety of motifs derived from classical sixteenth- and seventeenth-century Persian models.

Other Floral Motifs
In addition to their use as part of stylized design units, flowers are also seen as botanically recognizable elements, most notably in classical Mughal carpets. In a later group of Indian millefleurs prayer rugs, the mihrab is filled with an exuberant array of rose, poppy, tulip, carnation, and lily blossoms. Tulips and carnations are favored by Turkish weavers, and peonies, chrysanthemums, and lotuses are preferred by their East Turkestan, Tibetan, and Chinese counterparts.

Cloud Bands
Cloud-band motifs, which appear in both border and field designs, are Western imports via Chinese artisans brought to Samarkand in the fifteenth century by Mongol conquerors. From there, it migrated west and was soon adopted by Persian artists. Cloud bands are found in a variety of configurations in Persian, Turkish, Beshir Turkoman, and Far Eastern weavings.

Human and Animal Figures
The sayings attributed to Muhammad, the prophet of Islam, in the hadith forbid the representation of human figures. Some Muslim societies observe this stricture; others do not, but realistic figures are uncommon in all weaving groups except on pictorial carpets. Village rugs that include stick or cartoon-like men and women along with the domestic animals that share their lives and supply their larders are sure to bring a smile to a rug collector's face.

Realistic animals are found on classical Persian and Indian carpets, most notably on those known as "hunting rugs," but on village rugs they are reduced to block-like stylizations, stick figures, or abstractions. Among the wild animals seen on rugs are lions, an ancient symbol of strength and courage. Camels, horses, and birds are popular motifs in all weaving areas.

Top, Left. Stylized Motifs. Two versions of cloud bands.

Top, Right. Stylized Motifs. Human and animal figures seen on village and tribal rugs.

A wholly mythic figure is the dragon, pictured in a highly stylized form on early Caucasian carpets, which is thought to have originated from the Chinese winged-dragon symbols introduced along the East-West trade routes.

The Chinese repertoire of motifs also includes bats, symbolic of happiness; cranes for longevity; deer for well-being; and paired fish for abundance and prosperity. The fierce-looking foo dogs are symbols of a long and noble life.

Geometric Motifs

Many of the geometric designs seen on nineteenth-century rugs were derived from flower, leaf, and vine prototypes. On classical Turkish rugs, the realistic tulips and carnations beloved by Ottoman artists are used as both field and border motifs. Early Turkish rugs with geometric designs were so often used as

background decoration in the paintings by fifteenth-century European artists that some—such as Lorenzo Lotto, Hans Holbein, and Hans Memling—have been tagged with the artists' names.

Other motifs associated with the Turkish design tradition and used elsewhere by weavers with Turkic roots include:

Elibelinde
This motif, which means "woman with hands on hips," is a very old one said to symbolize fertility. It is often seen on Turkish kilims.

Ram's Horn
A male fertility symbol used both as a field motif and a border element.

Star

Stars indicate a wish for happiness and are used both boxed and unboxed as a repeat motif or in combination with other motifs.

Amulets

The comb-like motifs known as amulets appear in a variety of forms. They may serve a specific magical purpose, such as warding off evil, or simply be figures whose origin and meaning remain uncertain.

Gul

Gul, the Persian word for "rose," is applied primarily to octagons of varying proportions used as a repeat ornament in the rugs and trappings of nomadic Turkoman tribes who wandered westward from remote Asian steppes about two thousand years ago. The large primary guls identified with the various tribes were knotted as tribe-specific symbols only into rugs, and sometimes used by other tribes to decorate bags and other trappings. Secondary guls of lesser tribal significance were placed on the field of rugs at the point at which lines would intersect if drawn diagonally through the centers of the major guls in adjacent rows.

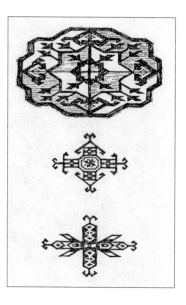

Geometric Motifs. Tekke major and minor guls.

Tekke

The major Tekke gul is always quartered by dark lines intersecting at right angles. There are two minor Tekke guls.

Yomud

The Yomud have three primary guls, only one of which, the kepse gul, is tribal specific. The use of secondary guls is inconstant. Yomud weavers tackled anything of a practical nature that could be woven, and their output was, and still is, very large.

Geometric Motifs. Bag face with Memling gul used as the central ornament.

Major Border Motifs. Kufic border variations.

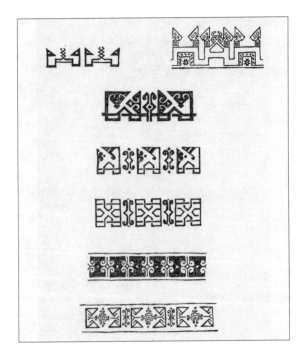

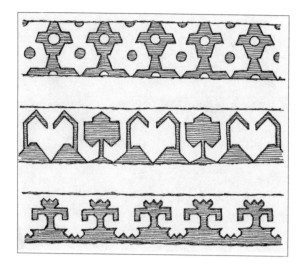

Major Border Motifs. Three versions of the reciprocal tulip/trefoil border motif.

Ersari

The largest of the Turkoman tribes, the Ersari commonly adopted designs from other sources to supplement their own clover leaf-like gulli-gul. Their weaving repertoire includes variations on the Mina Khani, cloud bands, and boteh.

Chodor

The primary Chodor gul, the ertmen, is a lozenge-shaped stepped gul containing stylized flowers and enclosed in a latticework.

Salor

The Salors were the most accomplished weavers among the Turkoman tribes. Their primary quartered gul contains three-stemmed clover-like figures in each quarter and a stylized animal figure. Another large crenelated gul appears only on weavings other than rugs.

Weavings that can be confidently attributed to the Salors are rare. Other tribes whose weavings lack easy identification are the Saryk, Arabatchi, and Kizil Ayak.

Memling Gul

A hooked, stepped figure similar to Turkoman guls that is seen on village and tribal rugs and bags

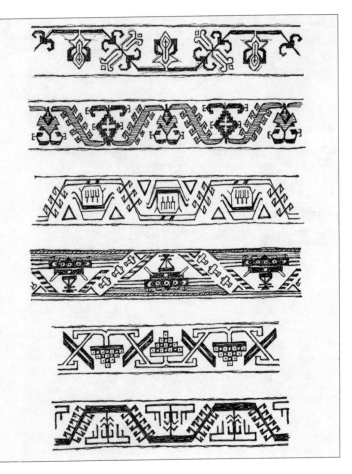

Major Border Motifs. Stylizations of the palmette and flowering vine border, including the Yomud "boat" border and a twentieth-century Soviet version transforming the original flower and vine forms into tanks and airplanes.

throughout the Middle Eastern weaving area. The name comes from the fifteenth-century Flemish painter, Hans Memling, whose paintings incorporated rugs with this design.

Major Border Motifs

Blossom and vine repeats—a design that appears in both the realistic and stylized forms of carnations, tulips, balsam, narcissuses, and, in Far Eastern rugs, lotuses and peonies.

Ram's horn—a very old Turkic symbol seen in everything from a simple hooked Y in minor borders, to more complex figures used in the borders of Turko-

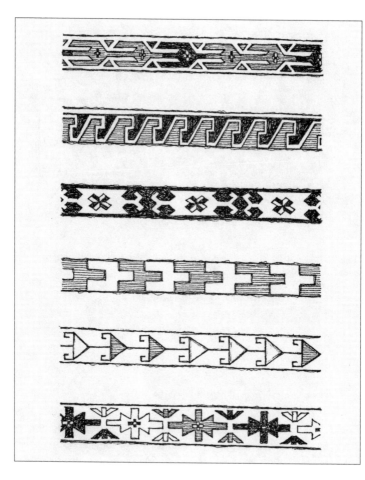

man, Turkish, and Kurdish tribal and village rugs. The end of the hooks may have a crested shape that some scholars claim are symbols for birds.

Ashik—a steeply stepped motif used by many Turkoman tribal weavers. Similar motifs are also seen on Turkish rugs.

Kufic—a variety of geometric main border designs based on a very old Arabic script known as Kufic.

Cloud band—borrowed from the Chinese weaving vocabulary, this popular border motif is often used in a humped version similar to a looped ribbon bow.

Minor Border Motifs. Minor border motifs, including "running dog."

Trefoil—a very old three-lobed reciprocal figure used in both major and minor borders.

Progression from flower and vine to boat—this interesting series of changes over the years occurs in Turkoman carpets. The realistic "boat border," seen in later pieces, was woven after the establishment of the Soviet Union in 1922.

Minor Border Motifs

The flower- and leaf-based repeats used for minor borders are usually highly stylized. An exception are the realistic carnations seen on some low-piled Caucasian rugs. Frequently used geometric motifs include diagonal barber-pole stripes, reciprocal sawtooths, angularized vines, and oblique-hooked oblique repeats often referred to as "running dog" or "latch hook."

Flat-Weave Motifs

The designs seen on flat-woven weavings tend to be dominated by repeat geometric patterns in horizontal, vertical, or diagonal rows. Banding is much more common than in pile rugs, and individual design units are often very large. Although curvilinear patterning is possible, as proven by the beautiful floral sixteenth-century Persian and Ottoman kilims and nineteenth-century Persian Senneh and Bidjar kilims, it is uncommon.

Stylized animals and birds are often seen on mixed-technique bags and other domestic articles. The plain-woven covers known as *verneh*, which typically boast brocaded parades of horses and camels, are much sought after by collectors of folk weaving. Caucasian soumaks featuring monumental S-shaped compartmented designs thought to be derived from the stylized dragons knotted into earlier carpets are also favored by collectors, a fact lost on neither dealers nor auctioneers. ◼

PART 2:
AN ORIENTAL
RUG OVERVIEW

5

CLASSICAL CARPETS & TRIBAL WEAVINGS, 1500–1800

Fine classical carpets and early tribal weavings are available only from a limited number of high-end dealers. Generally, they are consigned from long-standing private collections or as deacquisitions from museums to whichever of the major auction houses offer the best terms. Because of their extreme rarity, the condition of very old carpets and their fragments and tribal weavings has much less effect on prices than that of later rugs.

Turkish Double-Niche Prayer Rug

Bergama in western Anatolia (Turkey), second half of the seventeenth century. Wool warp and weft, 5'5" × 4'1". Palmettes connected with floral vines on a red field; white-bordered medallions in the dark blue spandrels; the wide red-ground border features palmettes within evenly spaced white, blue, and gold cartouches. *Photo from author's archives.*

Persian Shah Abbas Carpet

Mashad, sixteenth century. Wool pile with flat-woven silver thread on a cotton foundation, 11'6" × 18'3". Red field with Shah Abbas palmettes and graceful swirls of leafy vines; a blue major border with palmettes flanked by two flower-decorated yellow minor borders.

Photo from author's archives.

Indian Mughal Dynasty Long, Narrow Rug

Lahore, seventeenth century. Wool pile on a cotton foundation, 9'8" × 4'6". The red field has realistic iris, lily, rose, and narcissus plants arranged in a graceful sprawl on a red ground. Flowering plants are knotted in an orderly procession around a wide blue border flanked by gold minors. *Photo from author's archives.*

Chinese Ninghsia Carpet

Ninghsia, late eighteenth century. Wool pile on a cotton foundation, 5'3" × 12'1". Formal medallions and graceful peony clusters in blue are well spaced on an ivory field flanked by a Greek key–style red border and a wider blue border featuring pink peony blossoms.

Photo from author's archives.

Salor Turkoman Carpet

Sarakhs, northeast Iran, late eighteenth century. Wool pile on a wool foundation, 9' × 11'8". According to one expert, V. G. Moshkova, the Salors were "the most noble and aristocratic of the Turkmen tribes" and were known for the excellence of their weaving. This carpet features elegantly spaced Salor carpet guls in an infinite repeat on a brilliant scarlet ground surrounded by a simple geometric border. *Photo from author's archives.*

6

TRIBAL WEAVINGS, 1800–1925

Tribal weavings have a strongly traditional character associated with kinship groups and isolated, close-knit communities. Tribes that were once nomadic now live in villages during the winter and take their flocks to highland pastures in the summer. Although some of these articles were woven for sale or barter, most were made for domestic use.

Collectors of these articles accept the fact that because the looms used to weave them were both primitive and transportable, distortions are unavoidable. A deformed rug might not be suitable for a floor covering, but fifteen years ago a glowing but very skewed star Kazak sold at auction for $265,000. Mark Hopkins, a distinguished Boston collector, says that the

best tribal weavings offer "spontaneously inspired asymmetry . . . an altered dimension . . . a surprising cascade of animal or floral figures, an unexpected twist of line or form just at the point of tedium that transports a weaving to a subjective pinnacle of greatness."

Only knotted pile weavings are included here; flatwoven articles are listed under a separate heading later in this chapter.

Baluch Prayer Rug

Northeast Persia or western Afghanistan, late nineteenth century. Wool pile on a wool foundation. 2'7" × 4'7". Stylized tree-of-life on camel hair ground and dated hand panels. Minor borders with white rosettes frame the red on blue geometric main border. *Formerly in the author's collection. Photo from author's archives.*

Afshar Saddle Bags

South Persia, late nineteenth/early twentieth century. Wool pile on a wool foundation, 1' × 3'. Staggered rows of flattened botehs in blue, rose, camel, ivory, gold, and blue-green on a light red field bordered by a triple-leaf motif on blue. *Photo courtesy of Skinner, Inc.*

Yoruk Prayer Rug

East Anatolia (Turkey), early twentieth century. Wool
pile on a wool foundation, 2'9" × 4'9". Hooked comb-
like pendants in crimson, sky blue, gold, brown, and
blue-green on a rust red mihrab on a dark blue field
with stylized pitchers and combs within apricot geometric borders. *Photo courtesy of Skinner, Inc.*

Gabbeh Rug

Southwest Persia, early twentieth century. Wool pile on a wool foundation, 4'4" × 6' This name is applied to long-piled wool rugs with simple bold geometric motifs. Stepped concentric diamond medallions in red, dark blue, ivory, and blue-green on a gold field cornered with four male figures and bordered by arrowheads on ivory. *Photo courtesy of Skinner, Inc.*

Veramin Bag Face

North Persia, late nineteenth century. Wool pile on a wool foundation, 1'4" × 3'3". Precisely drawn Turko-man-style gul within an ivory medallion on a dark blue ground bordered by a stylized leaf-and-flower motif.

Photo courtesy of Skinner, Inc.

Khamseh Rug

Southwest Persia, late nineteenth century. Wool pile on a wool foundation, 3'6" × 5'10". Compressed tree-of-life motifs and rows of blossoming plants in red, slate blue, gold, and blue-green on a dark blue field within a charming ivory border populated with alert birds. *Photo courtesy of Skinner, Inc.*

Shahsavan Salt Bag

Northwest Persia, early twentieth century. Wool pile on a wool foundation, 1' × 1'7". The midnight blue field sports square medallions with ram's horn pendants in red, royal blue, gold, orange, and blue-green within an ivory geometric border. *Photo courtesy of Skinner, Inc.*

Tekke Asmalyk

Turkestan, early nineteenth century. Wool pile on a wool foundation, approximately 3' × 4'. One of a pair of decorative camel trappings with blue and ivory birds centered within four ivory and blue leaves on a red ground surrounded by a red curled-leaf border on ivory. *Photo from author's archives.*

7

VILLAGE RUGS, 1800–1925

Although made in a domestic setting and often used there, the village rugs being collected today were also an important source of family income. Originality was neither expected nor rewarded, but few weavers un-hampered by purely commercial interests could resist adding personal touches to tried and true designs, choosing an unusual combination of colors or using traditional motifs in untraditional ways.

Kazak Shield Rug

Southern Caucasus, late nineteenth century. Wool pile on a wool foundation, approximately 5' × 6'10". Bold ivory-bordered shield-like medallion with geometric motifs in red, gold, blue, green, and ivory on a red ground with boxed double ram's horns at each corner flanked by a gold floral minor border and a major border with boxed ram's horns and hooked gul-like figures. *Photo from author's archives.*

Shirvan Marasali Prayer Rug

Northern Caucasus, nineteenth century. Wool pile on a wool foundation, approximately 3' × 4'. Unusually widely spaced with meticulously detailed botehs in red, gold, blue, green, and ivory on an ivory ground mihrab bordered by a geometrized flower-and-vine border motif on red. *Photo courtesy of Skinner, Inc.*

Bergama Rug

Anatolia (Turkey), early nineteenth century. Wool pile on a wool foundation, 5' × 6'10". A boxed and pendanted central medallion in blue, ivory, and red on an ivory-dotted red ground with floral and star motifs. The ivory border has a stylized quatrefoil carnation motif in blue, red, coral, and cream on ivory. *Photo from author's archives.*

Tree Kazak Rug
Southwest Caucasus, late nineteenth century. Wool pile on a wool foundation, 5'9" × 8'. A vertical row of ivory-ground medallions flanked by large tree-of-life motifs in blue and ivory on a red ground bordered by octagons on a dark blue ground. *Photo courtesy of Skinner, Inc.*

Bahkshaish Rug

Northwest Persia, late nineteenth/early twentieth century. Wool pile on a wool foundation, 6' × 9'4". Bid majnun design featuring rows of blossoming trees, cypresses, and weeping willows in sky-blue, red, rose, camel, and blue-green on a dark blue field, bordered by palmettes and vines on rust. *Photo courtesy of Skinner, Inc.*

Bidjar Sampler

Northwest Persia, late nineteenth century. Wool pile on a wool foundation, approximately 4' × 5' This type of rug, which is a popular collector's item, showcases some of the formats, motifs, and natural-dye colors—in this case light red, gold, three shades of blue, salmon, ivory, and blue-green—used by the Kurdish weavers of Bidjar rugs. *Photo courtesy of Skinner, Inc.*

Hamadan Rug

Northwest Persia, early twentieth century. Wool pile on a wool foundation, 3'8" × 6'6". Imported by the hundreds into the United States, Hamadans are generally sturdy but undistinguished rugs. This one, with its columns of floral groups in red, sky-blue, red-brown, gold, green, and blue-green on a dark field is a standout thanks to well-proportioned borders and rich vegetable colors. *Photo courtesy of Skinner, Inc.*

Bahktiari Rug

Southwest Persia, early twentieth century. Wool pile on a wool foundation, 4'8" × 7'2". A nicely spaced example of a common Bakhtiari design with compartmented blossoming tree and other floral motifs in dark and medium blue, red, deep gold, ivory, and blue-green within a gold rosette and serrated leaf border. *Photo courtesy of Skinner, Inc.*

Konya Yastik

Central Anatolia (Turkey), second half of the nineteenth century. Wool pile on a wool foundation, 2' × 2'10". Yastiks are cushion covers popular with collectors. A central gul-like figure in aubergine, red, ivory, and blue is centered on an ivory medallion in a dark blue field bordered by stylized palmettes in ivory diamonds on a dark red ground. The tented ivory figures with leaf-like motifs on the end borders are known as lappets. *Photo from author's archives.*

8

FLAT WEAVES, 1800–1925

Bales of pile rugs used to be shipped wrapped in old kilims, which were once thought too humble to be of artistic or collectible interest. Today, the admirers of the bold designs and complex structures of the various types of flat weaves scornfully dismiss pile rugs as fussy "burr-cut stumps of yarn."

Turkish Kilim

West Anatolia (Turkey), early nineteenth century. Wool with ivory cotton highlights, approximately 5' × 9'. Three centered serrated medallions in gold, camel, light red, blue, and ivory on dark brown on a cream field flanked by long interlaced figures in light red and blue-green. *Photo from author's archives.*

Caucasion Shadda Cover

Karabagh, Caucasus, late nineteenth century. Wool brocading on wool plain weave, size unknown. Parades of camels in red, pale blue-green, ivory, and dark brown in two rows across a slate blue ground with midget-size horses placed horizontally between each camel. These pieces are sought after by collectors. *Photo courtesy of Skinner, Inc.*

Senneh Kilim

Northwest Persia, late nineteenth century. Finely woven wool kilim in a formal rug format, 4'4" × 6'8". Serrated dark blue medallion with matching spandrels on an ivory ground bordered with a floral motif on gold. *Photo courtesy of Skinner, Inc.*

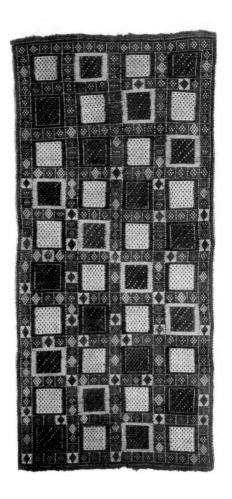

Caucasian Zili

Karabagh, Caucasus, late nineteenth century. Wool brocading on wool plain weave, 5'5" × 11'6". Typical pattern consisting of four evenly spaced rows of figured squares separated by narrow rows of diamond motifs in light and dark red, three shades of blue, gold, and ivory. *Photo courtesy of Skinner, Inc.*

Dragon Verneh

Karabagh, Caucasus, late nineteenth century. Plain weave wool patterned all over by extra weft wrapping, fragment, size unknown. The gigantic S-shaped blocks are said to be derived from the dragon figures on early Caucasian carpets. Red, dark and medium blue, gold, and ivory. *Photo courtesy of Skinner, Inc.*

Shirvan Kilim Saddle Bags

East Caucasus, late nineteenth century. Wool warp and weft, 1'6" × 3'6". Rows of dark blue and red radiating diamonds on an ivory field enclosed by a red, green, and dark brown zigzag border. *Photo courtesy of Skinner, Inc.*

9

COMMERCIAL DECORATIVE RUGS AND CARPETS

Most of the rugs made between 1875 and 1930, which are categorized as commercial furnishing pieces, were made in Persia (after 1935, Iran), but workshops in Turkey, India, and China were also busy during this period. The fact that the rugs they made were reproduced in large quantities in a range of popular sizes matters little to someone wanting no more than a handsome floor covering. The best of them, distinguished by the attention given to detail by the artists designing them and the skill of the weavers, are justly highly valued. The quirky variations in home-loomed rugs that appeal to collectors are considered unacceptable in workshop products.

When shopping for a decorative carpet, be aware that the word "quality" is used by the rug trade to grade the fineness of weave. It is a descriptive rather than a judgmental term. Given a group of rugs made of equally good materials, the more coarsely woven a rug, the lower the quality, even though the more finely knotted rugs may not, in fact, wear as well.

Kerman Prayer Rug

Southeast Persia, mid-nineteenth century. Wool pile on a cotton foundation, 3'2" × 6'. The ivory mihrab contains realistic iris plants flanking a blue vase with sprays of flowers in which two birds perch. The dark

blue spandrels have a graceful tracery of cochineal red vines, and flowers and vines fill the wide ivory border. Colors include pale and dark blue, yellow, soft red, medium brown, and ivory. *Photo from author's archives.*

Kansu Rug with Foo-Dogs

Northwest China, twentieth century. Wool pile on a cotton foundation, 5'5" × 8'. Foo-dogs in dark and light blue, pale yellow, and red frolic on a salmon ground bordered in a yellow-and-salmon braided motif and a wider outer border of cloud bands on light red. *Photo courtesy of Skinner, Inc.*

Mahal Carpet

West Persia, late nineteenth/early twentieth century. Wool pile on a cotton foundation, 8'7" × 11'6". The ivory field has an overall Mina Khani floral lattice in red, dark and light blue, rose, dark gold, and teal. Palmettes, rosettes, and curved leaves ornament the dark blue main border. *Photo courtesy of Skinner, Inc.*

Sarouk Ferahan Rug

West Persia, late nineteenth century. Wool pile on a cotton foundation, 4'4" × 6'8". These delicately patterned rugs predate the detached floral Sarouks with painted maroon fields that flooded the United States from 1920 to 1950. This example has a classic formal format on an ivory field with blue spandrels and a palmette and vine blue main border. *Photo courtesy of Skinner, Inc.*

Serapi Carpet

Northwest Persia, last quarter of the nineteenth century. Wool pile on a cotton foundation, 9'7" × 13'4". Ivory-centered medallion with pairs of blue and red leaves on a red flower- and leaf-decorated field, with ivory and dark blue spandrels. The dark blue main border has palmettes interconnected by vines and floral sprays. Colors include pale and dark blue, light red, pink, blue-green, and ivory. *Photo courtesy of Skinner, Inc.*

Serab Long Rug

Northwest Persia, early twentieth century. Wool pile on a wool foundation, 4'3" × 9'6". Two hexagonal medallions in midnight blue, red, rose, and blue-green on a latticework camel and ivory field. The main blue border has a variety of stylized floral and geometric motifs. *Photo courtesy of Skinner, Inc.*

Senneh Carpet

Northwest Persia, late nineteenth century. Wool pile finely knotted on a cotton foundation, 10'8" × 14'4". Stylized central medallion and pendants in blue on an abrashed red ground with geometrized palmettes in blue, ivory, and red on gold. The main blue border has a stylized palmette and flower repeat. *Photo courtesy of Skinner, Inc.*

NOTE: Please consult the Resource Guide for books and book dealers offering detailed information about the class of rugs that interest you the most.

10

CONTEMPORARY COLLECTIBLE RUGS

The cheap, easily applied synthetic dyes introduced into Middle Eastern rug weaving areas during the last quarter of the nineteenth century precipitated a decline in the prices wholesalers were willing to pay for rugs dyed with these garish, unstable colors, no matter how expertly woven. Dealers who prided themselves on stocking only natural-dye antique rugs searched in vain for new rugs they could offer with a clear conscience. The weaving craft, however, continued to be practiced and taught, and in 1981 the long overdue return to the use of natural dyes and handspun lanolin-rich wool was pioneered by DOBAG, a Turkish acronym that stands for Natural Dye Research and Development Project.

DOBAG

Dr. Harold Bohmer, a German chemist and rug scholar, provided the technical expertise for the villager-owned DOBAG cooperatives in northwestern Turkey. The designs are inspired by those surviving in rugs given over many years to local mosques, but the weavers choose the combination of motifs and colors of the rugs they make. DOBAG rugs have not been given any kind of chemical or aging treatment. Time alone enhances the sheen of the hard-wearing long-staple wool and mellows the rich vegetable colors.

Return to Tradition, an attractive retail outlet opened by Bill McDonnell in San Francisco in 1989, is the primary DOBAG dealership in the United States. McDonnell and another California dealer, Christopher Wahlgren of Nomad Rugs, also stock kilims woven by a small family-run cottage industry in Konya, Turkey, and in the Toros Mountain villages. *HALI* magazine has called Mehmet Ucar, its production head, "the master of the natural-dyed Konya kilim." Examples of DOBAG rugs and the Toros kilims can be viewed in color on the Return to Tradition website; Ucar's pile rugs and kilims may be seen at www.nomadrugs.com. DOBAG rugs average $65 per square foot; the kilims range from approximately $26 to $32 per square foot, depending on the complexity of the pattern. Specific information can be found at the end of this chapter.

Woven Legends

Inspired by the DOBAG project's commitment to natural dyes, George Jevremovic, a young American dealer in old rugs and kilims, began his own Turkish production with traditional Anatolian designs, but soon added new "folk art" influenced motifs and aesthetically pleasing variations on the sophisticated decorative designs sought by interior decorators. His first Azeri carpets were enthusiastically received in the United States and favorably compared to their antique forebears.

DOBAG.
Husbands of
DOBAG weavers
proudly
displaying rugs.
Photo courtesy
of Gayle Garrett.

Woven Legends owns the whole production process
in Turkey from wool, to dye plants, to loom. In 1989,
a joint venture called Black Mountain Looms was
formed, some of whose lines are made in China
and India. Today, Woven Legends has ten production
lines, which are described and illustrated on its website.

In addition to rug production, Jevremovic, in partner-
ship with Teddy Sumner, has developed two retail
outlets, one in Philadelphia, his home base, and the
other in Chicago. Known as Material Culture, they
offer rugs, pillows, folk and tribal art, textiles and pot-
tery, and eighteenth-, nineteenth-, and early twentieth-
century furniture from a wide variety of geographical
sources.

There is also a well-regarded Woven Legends restoration facility in Izmir, Turkey, whose prices, including
shipping, are significantly cheaper than in the West.
Details can be found in the Resource Guide.

Yayla Tribal Rugs and the Cultural Survival Rug Projects

In the course of work pursued in Pakistan among the rug-weaving refugees of the Afghan-Soviet war, Chris Walter, a Massachusetts-based rug dealer and scholar, determined that there was a need for a rug project similar to DOBAG to provide a crucial source of income and to maintain cultural identity.

As a result, there are currently three distinct aspects to Walter's operation: Yayla Tribal Rugs, a for-profit dealership founded in 1981; Barakat, Inc., a nonprofit corporation founded in 2000 for the purpose of channeling Yayla profits to other rug-weaving peoples; and Cultural Survival, a separate nonprofit organization that is dedicated to the protection of endangered peoples and cultures.

The Ersari Turkoman Weaving Project, whose rugs are made with hand-carded, hand-spun, long-staple wool dyed with traditional vegetable-derived dyes, was established in 1988 with start-up funds provided by Cultural Survival. In 1990, Cultural Survival funded a similar project to provide financial support to the Tibetan communities living in exile in Nepal. It is perhaps the only Tibetan rug venture still exclusively using vegetable dyes. Today, rugs with contemporary patterns as well as age-old, uniquely Tibetan designs and motifs are being woven with the long-staple, lanolin-rich wool typical of sheep reared in high-altitude grasslands. ◙

PART 3:
COLLECTIBLE RUG MARKET

11

A SAMPLING OF CURRENT MARKET PRICES

As recently as ten years ago, unless one lived in an urban center the search for a good oriental rug was both money and time intensive. Today, most dealers have a website featuring both old and new rugs in excellent, true-to-wool color. A very small sampling is presented in these pages but a trip to the Internet market to choose a rug and have it sent to you on approval is but a mouse click away.

If a visit to a dealer's shop suits you better, please call first to check on the hours the shop will be open and if the dealer has what you are looking for in stock.

The first four rugs are Persian antiques in excellent condition. The last piece is an antique Turkish kilim:

Shirvan rug

C. 1880, 3'10 x 6'5". Offered at $6,000 by John Collins Gallery, Newburyport, Massachusetts. *Photo courtesy of John Collins Gallery.*

Bidjar medallion rug
Late nineteenth century, 7' × 13'. Offered at $30,000 by
Peter Pap Oriental Rugs, Dublin, New Hampshire. *Peter
Pap Oriental Rugs. Photo courtesy of Don Tuttle.*

Serapi carpet
Late nineteenth century, 9' × 12'. Offered at $35,000 by Peter Pap Oriental Rugs, Dublin, New Hampshire. *Peter Pap Oriental Rugs. Photo courtesy of Don Tuttle.*

Aydin kilim
Late nineteenth century, 5'1" × 11'8", #K0000951. Offered
at $2,300 by Kilim.com, www.kilim.com. *Photo courtesy of
Kilim.com.*

The following rugs are new and made with hand-spun wool and natural dyes:

From Woven Legends' Euphrates Collection, retailing for between $80 and $100 per square foot:

Serapi carpet

9'6" × 12'10", EP 4116 500. *Photo courtesy of Woven Legends.*

Harshang and palmette patterned long rug

6'7" × 12'6", EP 44022R07 (see www.wovenlegends
.com for more information about the Woven Legends
collections and the dealers who carry them). *Photo courtesy of Woven Legends.*

Toros medallion kilim

5' × 7' from the Mehmet Ucar production near Konya, Turkey, KM 909116. Offered at $915 by William McDonnell of Return to Tradition, San Francisco, California. *Photo courtesy of Return to Tradition.*

DOBAG rug

5'3" × 8'6", DM87228Y1. Offered at $2,685 by William McDonnell of Return to Tradition, San Francisco, California. *Photo from author's archives.*

Turkish kilim

Konya, 4'2" × 6', K0000201. Offered at $440 by Kilim.com, www.kilim.com. *Photo courtesy of Kilim.com.*

12

CARE, REPAIR, AND MAINTENANCE

Wear caused by foot traffic and stains deposited by imperfectly trained pets exact a drastic toll on old oriental rugs. If you collect or inherit small items in good condition but have no sheltered floor space, consider either displaying them on a wall or tabletop. If made of silk, there is no good alternative. Used as a floor furnishing, a silk rug will soon display signs of wear. But whether old or new, even the sturdiest rug should be supplied with a pad, the type depending on its size, weight, and placement.

A large rug bearing the weight of heavy furniture or placed in a dining room where it will be subjected to the repeated sliding of chairs and feet requires a dense firm pad.

Scatter and lightweight rugs placed on waxed wood floors are accidents waiting to happen. In this situation, a nonskid underlayment is essential to protect family and guests from injurious falls. Please do not attempt to anchor rugs by tacking them directly into the floor or by pasting nonskid strips onto their backs.

Oriental runners provide a pleasing accent for a graceful stairway, but rugs chosen for this purpose should be tightly woven and free from splits and creases that heels could catch in. Whether installed with or without an underlayment, stair runners should be secured at the back of each step with a rod designed to allow it to give a bit with the push and pull of stairway traffic.

Although a pad cannot prevent heavy furniture from denting rugs, it will serve to buffer the abrasive action of grit and uneven flooring. And no matter what the size or material of a rug used as a floor covering, rotating it 180 degrees every six months will help distribute wear.

Types of Underlayments

The dimensions of a rug pad should be the same as the rug minus one inch. Exclude fringes from your measurements, except for Turkoman or Baluch rugs with decorated flat-woven skirts.

Durable underlayments for use between rugs and hard-surfaced floors include:

Rug Anchor II, a solid rubber sheeting available in one-eighth- and one-quarter-inch thickness, and Gridlock, a one-eighth-inch-thick openwork "waffle" pattern cushion. Neutral color, clean, odorless, and long lasting. For more information and dealer locations, contact Jade Industries, 837 Sussex Blvd., Broomall, PA 19008, tel. 610-328-1010, 888-RUG-PADS, fax 610-328-3306, e-mail: jade@rugpads.com, website: www.rugpads.com.

DuraHold, a one-quarter-inch-thick synthetic fiber that is bonded to a solid waffle-patterned rubber backing. Grayish-brown color, sturdy, and moisture and mildew resistant. Good choice for large heavy rugs. Call 800-227-7237 for a dealer nearest you.

Underlayments designed to prevent the movement of rugs placed on carpeting include:

Wedlock, by Jade Industries. A thin white synthetic material coated on both sides with a nontransferable, nonmarring adhesive. Trim to size, then peel off protective film. Available in rolls or precut sizes.

Miracle Hold, Leggett & Platt, Vantage Industries. Similar to Wedlock. Trim to size, then peel off plastic backing. This very effective, reasonably priced product is available at many stores in prepackaged standard sizes under different names: Ethan Allen, Magic Hold; JCPenney, Miracle Hold; K-Mart, Wonderhold; Kohl's, Rug Tact; Lowe's, Carpet Grabber; Menards, Double Grip; Target, Magic Hold; and Wal-Mart, Hold Over.

No-Muv, a dense rigid product with a toe-stubbing thickness (one-half inch) that makes it more suitable for large rugs and carpets than scatters and mats. Call 800-227-7237 for a dealer nearest you.

Wall Displays

Large carpets are poor choices for wall display. The considerable effort involved in hanging one makes it easy to postpone taking it down, but over time a heavy carpet hanging unsupported except at the top edge will noticeably sag. In fact, depending on the degree of stretch it may be impossible to restore it to its original dimensions.

Since warps are stronger than wefts, old rugs chosen for wall display should be hung vertically. If the design or the wall space demands otherwise, the display period should be limited.

Velcro Display System

At least a few of the fine old rugs a collector prizes will have skewed dimensions that tend to make them ripple to a greater or lesser degree when hung. Accordingly, a rug suspended from rings or hooks often presents an untidy appearance unless fussed with at tedious length, and because of the unequal stress on the warps it will eventually develop scallops between the suspension points.

The easiest way to achieve aesthetically pleasing wall displays is with Velcro fastening tape. Velcro is most commonly available in black, white, and beige and in widths varying from three-eighths to two inches. Staple or tack the hooked strip to a wooden batten cut to the width of the widest rug you intend to display, and secure it with attachments determined by the wall's construction, that is, wood frame, brick, or concrete.

Attach the fluffy Velcro strip to the top edge of the rug with stout button thread of a similar color. (If the weave is tight, you will need a sharp strong needle and a pair of small pliers to pull it through.)

Attach the rug to the wall mount by firmly pressing the tapes together. If the rug hangs unevenly—it probably will at first—pull the Velcro strips apart here and there to make the necessary adjustments. For maximum positioning flexibility, use a two-inch Velcro strip on the wall mount.

Lining
If a rug is left hanging for long periods, it should be lined to discourage insects from settling in. A used, well-washed bed sheet is an ideal choice for this purpose in terms of weight, stability, and texture. Thrift shops can usually supply one.

After cutting the sheet to size, tack it along the top and sides of the rug with large loose stitches. Hang the rug for a few days to see if any puckering develops. After making necessary adjustments, the bottom may be tacked into place.

Displaying Fragments
Rug fragments and bag faces hung "as is" look rather forlorn. The same piece stitched or Velcroed onto a fabric-covered panel achieves distinction. The object

is to create a smooth matte surface held tight to the wall yet projecting sufficiently to create a vertical stage set apart from it. For home display, a piece of Homasote or particleboard smoothly sheathed in fabric is more appropriate than a picture frame. If you choose a neutral color for the panel covering, bear in mind that the white and ivory portions of old rugs are apt to be a lot darker than one realizes, and if placed against too pale a background will look drab and dirty rather than antique. If you plan to use Velcro, take a test piece with you when choosing a fabric to be sure the surface is fuzzy enough to connect with the hooked side of the tape. (Note that a second pair of hands will be needed to help you mount the fabric because it is impossible for one person to keep it sufficiently taut while stapling the folded ends onto the panel's back.)

Lighting

Artful lighting enhances the luster and color of a rug's pile and the elegance and charm of its design. In fact, this effect is so pronounced it is advisable never to bid on any lot unexamined during an auction sale's preview. The flaws in rugs seen at a distance under theatrical lighting can be easily overlooked.

Museum lighting is severely limited because of concern about the long-term effect of strong light on colors and fibers. Collectors concerned about the illumination of their wall displays can install dimmers and reserve the highest level of light for special occasions.

Rug Storage

Rugs you plan to store, whether seasonally or for longer periods of time, should first have any food-spill remains removed and then be thoroughly vacuumed on both the front and back.

1. Make a note of the rugs' placement on your floors so that the direction can be reversed when they are next put down. This helps distribute wear more evenly.

2. Rugs should be rolled with the pile inward and in the direction of the pile to avoid crushing and crimping

the fiber. (Run your palm over the surface: the smooth feel is with the pile, the rough feel is against it.)

3. Do not fold a large rug before rolling. This will create unsightly creases difficult to remove and may crack an old, dry foundation. The reason dealers roll large carpets into squat cylinders is to make them easily accessible for frequent display.

4. Do not wrap rolled rugs in plastic! Plastic seals in moisture, which promotes mildew and, if a rug is cotton-wefted, dry rot. Either make a tube of closely woven fabric—for example, one of those thrift shop sheets—or use heavy brown wrapping paper sealed with tape. Whatever the type of wrapping, rugs should first be treated with one of the insect repellents discussed later on.

Storage Problems

Cellars, garages, and attics lacking ventilation should be avoided as storage areas. Cellars tend to be damp and attics excessively hot. Leaky attics and garages, which alternate between being too damp and too dry, compound the problems. Sunlight and air will stop the growth of mildew, and even though dry rot—a microscopic plant-like fungus that feeds on cellulose fibers—can be arrested, already infected fibers will eventually crack and disintegrate when subjected to stress. Silk fibers may shatter if rugs containing a significant amount of silk are stored in hot unventilated attics.

Control of Rug-Damaging Insects

The two most common clothes moths look very much alike. When adult, both are small, yellowish-buff in color, and flit erratically. The webbing moth spins a silky coverlet under which its white, dark-headed larvae feed and pupate. Case-making moths construct a small portable case from the woolen material they feed on. When the feeding stage ends, the pupating larvae attaches its case in a protected place.

In many areas, carpet beetles cause the damage to rugs attributed to moths. These small oval beetles may be solid black or mottled with white, brown, or yellow. Their larvae, which measure from one-quarter- to one-half-inch long, depending on the species, have bristles ending in tufts of long hairs. After feeding on pollen and vegetable matter, the adult female beetles fly through any available opening in buildings to deposit their eggs. Infestations of beetle larvae have decimated museum collections of insects, wool textiles, and the hides and fur of mounted animals.

Before wrapping rugs for storage, sprinkle them with paradichlorobenzene flakes or crystals at the U.S. Department of Agriculture recommended rate of at least 1 pound per 100 cubic feet of space. Paradichlorobenzene vapors have the added advantage of deterring mildew. (Although naphthalene moth balls and crystals are more easily available, naphthalene is not as effective and some conservators suspect that long-term use of it may cause color changes in rug dyes.)

Even rugs in actively used rooms can harbor destructive insects. If you discover any adults or their larvae on a rug, vacuum it thoroughly front and back and follow up with a room fogger formulated to kill the insects causing the trouble.

Repair, Restoration, and Conservation
An informed decision about the correct approach to a given rug requires answers to at least three basic questions:

1. Will the historic and/or market value of the repaired rug compensate for the cost of professional repair?

2. Does its decorative or sentimental value outweigh monetary considerations?

3. Should stopgap home repairs be attempted if the cost of a proper repair must be postponed?

Functional Repairs
At its best, functional repair approaches restoration. Fiber type, weight, ply, and color are closely matched to the original warp, weft, and pile, and when com-

pleted, the repaired area should be hard to detect except on close examination. Work of this quality is pricey. Low-end stitch-and-patch repairs are acceptable only for rugs that have suffered irreversible damage but can still function as furnishing pieces.

Restoration

Expert restorers will spend as much time studying a rug's structure, colors, and fibers as they do in weaving and knotting. As veteran restorer Rebecca Venable once said, "rugs are not ruined in a day or restored overnight." A restoration worthy of the name virtually duplicates the original weaving. Custom dying and hand spinning may be required to achieve as exact a match as possible.

True restoration is extremely expensive, but owners of an exceptional classic carpet or rug that represents tribal design and weaving at its characteristic best should think of it as an investment. During an economic downturn, the finest examples of any of the arts often increase in value at the same time that the prices of merely good ones reflect the stock market's decline.

Conservation

Repair and restoration necessitates the removal of original materials and the addition of new ones, which in effect destroys the information inherent in the piece's original structure. Even a worn and damaged piece with little market value might be a worthy candidate for conservation. For example, the mat your great-aunt's spaniel slept on might be a type of tribal weaving of which only a very few examples are represented in Western collections. Ideally, any repairs made either by you or a professional to weavings providing an important clue to the progression of design or use of color should be reversible.

Taste and opinions change in rugs as they do in everything else, and judging from some of the rugs prized in the past, it isn't easy to predict what a future generation will consider beautiful or important.

Simple Home Repairs

This section will outline a few simple ways to arrest the fraying of edges and the loss of pile, but please consider the following before you begin:

1. Edge and end repairs are painstaking tasks requiring the kind of temperament unbothered by the repetitious duplication of small details.

2. An irreversible action can do more harm than good. Unlike a frame on a picture, a rug's edges and ends are an integral part of its structure. A frayed weft thread here and a lost pile knot there can be compared to that missing shoe on the messenger's horse that led to the loss of the battle.

That said, it isn't difficult to do basic repairs as long as you allow the rug to guide you. Remove as little of the original materials as possible, but if the only yarn you have on hand when you have a couple of hours free for a stopgap repair is magenta acrylic, use it! Either you or a professional repair person can replace it with a more suitable yarn at a later date.

Materials for Home Repairs

1. Large-eyed sharp and blunt-ended tapestry needles

2. Thimble

3. Small pliers for pulling needles through rug foundations

4. Tweezers for removing pile knots and damaged edge overcastings

5. Small scissors

6. Wooden mallet for flattening new edge overcastings

7. Kitchen matches for singeing the fuzz from new overcastings

8. Linen thread or much less costly button and carpet threads in beige, brown, dark red, and medium blue

9. Wool yarns matched as closely as possible to your clean rug from the wide range of colors available in

shops specializing in needlepoint supplies; if the rug is too large to haul in for matching, try using paint sample cards

Note that pile colors are matched to the cut end of needlepoint yarns. For flat-weave repairs, match the original to a flat-lying strand.

Pile Rugs

An alternative to pile replacement in very worn rugs is a technique known as kashmiring, which is a type of darning in which wool yarns are carried around exposed warps in a figure-eight stitch. This can be used as a simple wrapping stitch to strengthen worn areas adjacent to the edges or chained around foundation threads where the pile is either very worn or missing. The effect of kashmiring is largely cosmetic and should not be thought of as a substitute for a well-executed repair. Its success depends on how well the colors of the yarns are matched to the rug.

Edge Repairs

The replacement of the broken or loose fibers overcast around a rug's edge warps can be successfully done at home by matching the color and density of the repair yarns as closely as possible and copying the tension and angle of the existing adjacent fibers. Blend the repaired edge into the original by passing a lighted match over the fuzz, then pound the plump new yarn flat with a mallet.

If sections of the edge warp cords have separated from the wefts extending from the rug's foundation and woven into or around them, take the time to examine closely the weft-weaving technique used to secure the edge cords to the foundation before proceeding further.

Thread a large-headed needle with a thread matched to the original weft color. Insert the needle into the back of the rug, run it through up to eight sound warps, then depending on the number of cord-bundles along the edge, loop the thread over and under them before returning the needle and thread

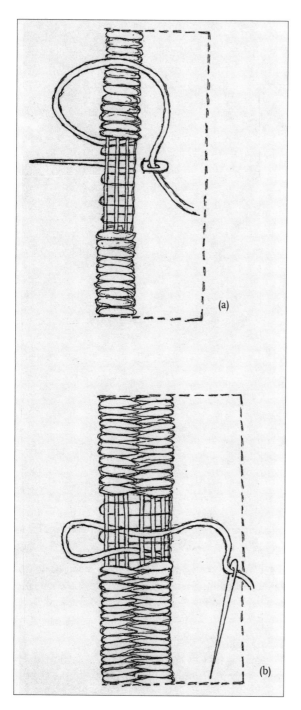

Edge Repairs.
(a) Securing a single bundle of edge warp cords into the foundation of a rug and (b) overcasting exposed edge warp cords.

(a)

(b)

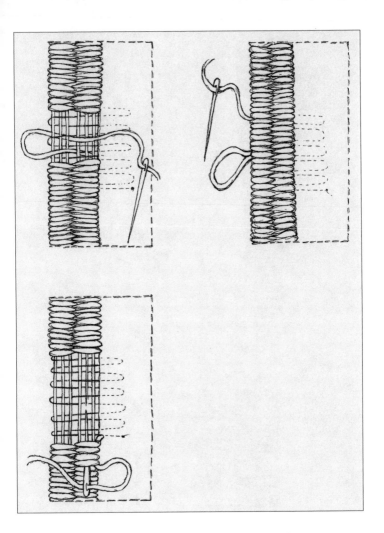

Edge Repairs. Securing and overcasting an edge consisting of two bundles of warp cords.

through sound warps into the body of the rug. Try to reproduce the original tension as closely as possible.

If sections of the warp cords are severely frayed, broken, or missing, it would be best to seek the services of a professional repair person. Recommendations are included in the Resource Guide.

False Edgings

The application of a false edging or machine overcasting is not recommended for collectible weavings.

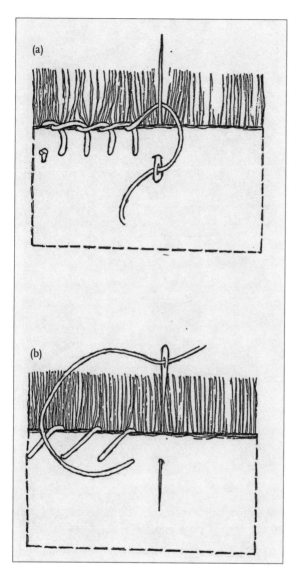

Ends. Securing rug ends with overcasting: (a) the right way and (b) the wrong way.

While acceptable for older worn furnishing rugs, be aware that false edging, which is sewn onto rather than into the rug's foundation, may require reinforcement from time to time to prevent it from pulling loose from the warps to which it is precariously attached.

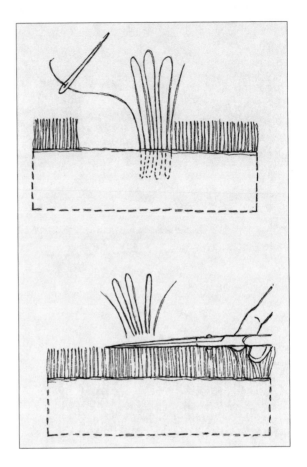

Ends

Unless the warps have been securely netted or braided, the ends of all oriental rugs should be securely overcast to prevent the unraveling of wefts and loss of pile knots.

If a section of fringe has been cut, torn, or chewed off, new threads matched as closely as possible in density and color to the original can be anchored into the foundation, then trimmed and the ends teased out with an old toothbrush.

Manufactured Fringes

A fringe sewn to the end of the rug presents the same problem as false edgings. Unless the rug is placed in an out-of-the-way area, the stress of foot traffic may pull it loose, taking with it the wefts and pile knots to which it was attached.

Rug Painting

The conservative view is that painting is never acceptable. The painting of a worn rug by unscrupulous dealers intending to deceive unknowing customers is, of course, indefensible. But there are some cases where it makes a good deal of practical sense:

1. Old repairs made with wool whose colors have faded over time

2. Spots bleached noticeably paler than the surrounding pile

3. The bright white tufts that sometimes work up through the pile from cotton foundations (Sanford permanent markers can also be used for this purpose)

4. Worn rugs possessing little or no market value but which could, with freshened colors or partially repainted designs, continue to serve as decorative floor coverings

The most satisfactory coloring agent for home use is acrylic paint used as watercolor. When the water evaporates, it leaves behind a thin layer of flexible, waterproof, and virtually fade-proof film of color. Starter kits are widely available, and one of these plus a few tubes of gray or brown shades for muting should prove sufficient. Avoid using white: it tends to make the colors chalky.

In addition to the paint, you'll need a couple of stubby brushes, some cotton swabs for mixing, a medicine dropper for dispensing water, and some small shiny white plates for mixing. Always mix and match the colors in daylight, and work fast. One, two, or three coats, separated by drying, may be required. Always wash your brushes with soap and water immediately after use. ◼

RESOURCE GUIDE

AUCTION HOUSES

Butterfield & Butterfield
7601 Sunset Blvd.
Los Angeles, CA 94103
Tel: 415-503-3201

Christie's
Rockefeller Center
20 Rockefeller Plaza, 49th St.
New York, NY 10020
Tel: 212-636-2000
Website: www.christies.com

The Heritage on the Garden
63 Park Plaza
Boston, MA 02116
Tel: 617-350-5400
Los Angeles
360 North Camden Dr.
Beverly Hills, CA 90210
Tel: 310-385-2600

Skinner, Inc.
357 Main St.
Bolton, MA 01740
Tel: 978-779-6241
Website: www.skinnerinc.com

Sotheby's
1334 York Ave. at 72nd St.
New York, NY 10021
Tel: 212-606-7000
Website: www.sothebys.com

CARPET CLEANING, REPAIR, RESTORATION, AND SUPPLIES

Advanced Restorations, Inc.
Ken Koets
Grand Rapids, MI 49504
Tel: 616-454-2222
Fax: 616-454-2249
E-mail: handwash@iserv.net

Antique Rug Co.
Barry Amiri
928 North La Cienega Blvd.
Los Angeles, CA 90069
Tel: 310-659-3847
Fax: 310-659-2288
E-mail: bamiri@pacbell.net
(Offering a full range of services relating to old and antique carpets)

Auserehl & Company
PO Box 1106, 565 3rd St.
Berthoud, CO 80513
Tel: 800-795-5384
Fax: 208-263-2589
E-mail:
info@orientalrugcleaning.com
Website:
www.orientalrugcleaning.com

Barsamian Oriental Rugs
Ed Barsamian
102 Madison Ave.
New York, NY 10016
Tel: 212-689-6273

Certified Cleaning & Restoration
Paul Brown
5670 Dempset Place
Santa Rosa, CA 95403
Tel: 707-322-7208
E-mail: cydyn@aol.com

Chatalbash Rug Co., Inc.
20 East 30th St.
New York, NY 10016
Tel: 212-532-5260
E-mail: chatalbashrug@aol.com
(Complete line of rug repair and cleaning supplies; catalog on request)

Danny and Sabrina Livai
13552 Deerwater Dr.
Germantown, MD 20874-2844
Tel: 301-515-0476

Emmanuel's Rug and Upholstery Cleaners
Thea M. Sand
1105 Rainier Ave.
South Seattle, WA 98144
Tel: 206-322-2200
E-mail: emmrug@qwest.net

Hanna Ayoub Oriental Rug Cleaning Company
5213 Wisconsin Ave. NW
Washington, DC 20015
Tel: 202-363-9200

Hayko Restoration & Conservation
Hayko Oltaci
857 Lexington Ave. at 65th St., 2nd Fl.
New York, NY 10021
Tel: 212-717-5400
Fax: 212-717-2783
E-mail: info@hayko.com
Website: www.hayko.com

Holly Lorraine Smith & Co.
1060 High Street
Dedham, MA 02026
Tel: 781-326-5200
Website: www.hollysmithrugs.com
(Rugs, tapestries, and textiles)

Jahnava's Oriental Rug Restoration and Cleaning
Jahnava Jenkins and Fayaz Ahamed
221 Pine St.
Florence, MA 01062
Tel: 413-585-9475

Kavanroodi, Shahriar
6110 Harleston Dr.
Atlanta, GA 30328
Tel: 404-843-2217
E-mail: roodi@mindspring.com
Website: www.oldrugsonline.com

Mark Keshishian & Sons Oriental Carpets
4505 Stanford St.
Chevy Chase, MD 20815
Tel: 301-654-4044
Website: www.keshad.htm

McGee Keshishian
Harold Keshishian and Melissa Keshishian
15525 Edwards Ferry Rd.
Poolesville, MD 20837
Tel: 202-362-3303

Oldcarpet.com, Inc.
Afshin Nejad
PO Box 1031
Brea, CA 92822
Tel: 310-766-1820
Fax: 419-781-4735
Website: www.oldcarpet.com

Renaissance Rug & Textile Cleaning, Inc.
Randy Hyde
914 Southeast Stephens St.
Portland, OR 97214
Tel: 503-963-8565
(Specializing in hand washing and repair of rugs and textiles)

Robert Pittenger
158 West 23rd St.
New York, NY 10011
Tel: 212-691-6948
(Specializing in hand washing and repair of rugs)

Rug Renovating
532 North Grove St.
South Orange, NJ 07017
Tel: 973-675-8313
Website: abchomecare.com

Talisman Oriental Rug Cleaning and Restoration
719 Swift St. #10
Santa Cruz, CA 95060
Tel: 408-425-7847
(Exceptionally knowledgeable in all respects)

Textile Conservation Workshop, Inc.
Patsy Orlofsky
3 Main St.
South Salem, NY 10590
Tel: 914-763-5805
E-mail: textile@bestweb.net

Textile Conservators, Inc.
Maury Bynum
215 West Ohio, 8th Fl.
Chicago, IL 60610
Tel: 312-329-0097
E-mail: maurybynum
@textileconservators.com
Website: www.textileconservators.com

Tina Kane Textile Restoration & Conservation
8 Big Island Rd.
Warwick, NY 10990
Tel/Fax: 914-986-8522
E-mail: tinakane@mx1.pair.com

William A. Marshall
3415 East Kleindale Rd., Ste. 131
Tucson, AZ 85716
Tel: 520-326-9432
(A large modern cleaning plant)

Woven Legends Restoration, Inc.
Robert Mann
2540 Walnut St.
Denver, CO 80205
Tel: 303-292-9865
Fax: 303-292-9801
(Mann represents Woven Legends' full-service carpet restoration facility in the Aegean Free Zone in Izmir, Turkey)

RUG & CARPET DEALERS IN THE U.S.

Many of the dealer websites listed here are excellent. The color and detail closely approximate the real thing and make shopping for rugs at long distance much easier than it was in the recent past.

Arizona
David E. Adler Oriental Rugs
6990 East Main St.
Scottsdale, AZ 85251
Tel: 602-941-2995
(Contemporary as well as antique rugs)

George Fine Kilims
7850 North Silverbell Rd. #114-177
Tucson, AZ 85743
Tel: 520-682-6865
Fax: 520-616-8949
E-mail: george@finekilims.com
Websites: www.finekilims.com, www.tucsonbazar.com

Northern California
Accent on Rugs of Los Gatos
Philip Brouwer
10 Station Way
Los Gatos, CA 95030
Tel: 408-354-8820
Fax: 408-354-1804
Website: www.accentonrugs.com

Anne Halley
PO Box 2825
San Anselmo, CA 94979
Tel: 415-456-8971
Fax: 415-456-9197
(By appointment)

Carpets of the Inner Circle
Roger Cavanna
444 Jackson St.
San Francisco, CA 94111
Tel: 415-398-2988
E-mail: rumi@c-innercircle.com

Emmett Eiland Oriental Rug Co.
1326 9th St.
Berkeley, CA 94710
Tel: 510-526-1087, 888-811-7847
E-mail: erugs@internetrugs.com
Website:
www.internetrugs.com/home.html
(Selection of new and antique rugs)

Hazara Oriental Rug Co.
Mohammad R. Zavvar
6251 College Ave.
Oakland, CA 94618
Tel: 510-655-3511
Fax: 510-655-5223
E-mail: info@hazaragallery.com
Website: www.wenet.net/~hazara
(Particularly strong on nomadic and tribal weavings)

The James Blackmon Gallery

James Blackmon
2140 Bush St. #1
San Francisco, CA 94115
Tel: 415-922-1859
E-mail: jwb111@pacbell.net

Krimsa Fine Rugs & Decor

2190 Union Street,
San Francisco, CA 94123
Tel: 415-441-4321
Website: www.krimsa.com

Nomad Rugs

Christopher Wahlgren
3775 24th St.
San Francisco, CA 94114
Tel: 415-401-8833
Fax: 415-401-8855
E-mail: christopher@nomadrugs.com
Website: www.nomadrugs.com

Peter Pap Oriental Rugs
of San Francisco

470 Jackson St.
San Francisco, CA 94111
Tel: 415-956-3300
E-mail: info@peterpap.com
Website: www.peterpap.com

Return to Tradition

Bill McDonnell
3319 Sacramento St.
San Francisco, CA 94118
Tel: 415-921-4180
E-mail: rugs@dobag.com
Website: www.returntotradition.com
(Natural-dye Turkish pile rugs and
kilims)

Tahoe Rug Studio

George V. Postrozny
475 North Lake Blvd.
Tahoe City, CA 96145
Tel: 530-581-2555
E-mail: georgep@intercomm.com
(New natural-dyed rugs as well an-
tique tribal and room-size rugs)

Tony Kitz Oriental Carpets

2843 Clay St.
San Francisco, CA 94115-1716
Tel: 415-346-2100

Southern California
Brian Morehouse Oriental Carpets

Los Angeles, CA 90001
Tel: 323-939-2240
Fax: 213-931-4987
E-mail: Morehousebri@aol.com

Don Blatchford Carpets and Art

Don Blatchford
1302 Montana Ave.
Santa Monica, CA 90403
Tel: 310-451-9008
E-mail: blatc7474@aol.com
Website: www.donblatchford.com

The Rug Warehouse

3260 Helms Ave.
Los Angeles, CA 90034
Tel: 310-838-0450, 800-659-6755
Fax: 310-838-3868
E-mail: info@therugwarehouse.com
Website: www.therugwarehouse.com
(New and antique rugs, and a direct
importer of natural-dyed hand-spun
yarn rugs from Peshawar, India, and
Nepal)

Keith Rocklin Oriental Rugs

Keith Rocklin
Los Angeles, CA
Tel: 310-203-8420
E-mail: krocklin@aol.com
(By appointment only; specialist in
collectible tribal rugs, bags, and tex-
tiles, including pre-Columbian)

Colorado

Isberian Rug Company
520 East Hyman Ave.
Aspen, CO 81611
Tel: 970-925-8062
Fax: 970-925-1381
300 East Cody Ln.
Basalt, CO 81621
Tel: 970-927-8541
Fax: 970-927-8233
E-mail: mindy@isberianrugs.com
Website: www.isberianrugs.com

Patrick Webb Oriental & Navajo Rug Co.
929 Main St.
Longmont, CO 80501
Tel: 303-772-7962
Fax: 303-772-9652.
E-mail: yastik@frii.com
Website:
www.orientalandnavajorugs.com

Robert Mann Oriental Rugs, Inc.
Robert Mann
2540 Walnut St.
Denver, CO 80205
Tel: 303-292-2522

Shaver-Ramsey Oriental Rugs
Paul Ramsey and Carolyn Shaver
2414 East 3rd Ave.
Denver, CO 80206
Tel: 303-320-6363
Fax: 303-320-1541
E-mail: info@shaver-ramsey.com
Website: www.shaver-ramsey.com
(A large selection of natural-dyed
rugs; see also KRIMSA in northern
California)

Connecticut
Oriental Rugs Ltd.
Ralph DiSaia and Karen DiSaia
23 Lyme St.
Old Lyme, CT 06371
Tel: 860-434-1167
E-mail: orientalrugs@snet.net

Tschebull Antique Carpets
Raoul (Mike) Tschebull
903 Post Rd.
Darien, CT 06820
Tel: 203-655-6610
Fax: 203-655-1379
E-mail: tschebull@sbcglobal.net
Website:
www.tschebullantiquecarpets.com
(Internationally recognized rug
scholar dealing exclusively in fine
old rugs)

Delaware
John D. Kurtz
1701 North Lincoln St.
Wilmington, DE 19806
Tel: 302-654-0442
E-mail: jkurtz45@aol.com
Website: www.newmooncarpets.com

District of Columbia
David Zahirpour Oriental
Rug Gallery
David Zahirpour
4922 Wisconsin Ave. NW
Washington, DC   20016-4104
Tel: 202-338-4141

Trocadero Textile Art
Bill Seward
2313 Calvert St. NW
Washington, DC 20008
Tel: 202-328-8440
(Old rugs and a good selection
from new natural-dyed productions)

Florida
Herat, Ltd.
Edward (Art) Koch
7024-G South West 114 Place
Miami, FL 33173
Tel: 305-412-0996
E-mail: ako@bellsouth.net
Website: www.herat.com

Silk Road Traders
Larry Tadross
3718 Southeast Ocean Blvd.
Stuart, FL 34994
Tel: 772-221-1767
Fax: 772-221-7858
E-mail: info@silk-road-traders.com
Website: www.silk-road-traders.com

Georgia
Afghanistan's Nomadic Rugs, Inc.
Tamor Shah
3219 Cains Hill Place NW
Atlanta, GA 30305
Tel: 404-261-7259
25 Bennett St.
Atlanta, GA 30309
Tel: 800-686-7030, 404-350-9560

Marla Mallett, Textiles
1690 Johnson Rd. NE
Atlanta, GA 30306
Tel: 404-872-3356
E-mail: marlam@mindspring.com
Website: www.marlamallett.com
(The attic gallery is open by appointment)

Idaho
Davies Reid
Heidi Davies and Terry Reid
140 Sun Valley Rd.
Ketchum, ID 83340
Tel/Fax: 208-726-3453
Website: www.daviesreid.com

Shabahang Persian Carpets
Roddy Yazdanpour and Johanna
de Jong
801 West Bannock St.
Boise, ID 83702
Tel: 800-269-0550
E-mail: info@shabahang-boise.com
Website: www.shabahang-boise.com

Illinois
Connoisseur Oriental Rugs
Mo Jamali
1000 Chicago Ave.
Evanston, IL 60202
Tel: 847-866-6622

Minasian Oriental Rugs
Carnig A. Minasian
1244 Chicago Ave.
Evanston, IL 60202
Tel: 847-864-1010
Fax: 847-492-4612

The Oriental Rug Mart
Jim Demanes
1916 North Knoxville Ave.
Peoria, IL 61603
Tel: 309-688-5005
Fax: 309 682-9634
E-mail: jimrug1@aol.com
Website: www.demanesrug.com
(Fourth-generation family business)

Indiana
Aaron's Oriental Rug Gallery
Bob Anderson
1217 Broadway
Ft. Wayne, IN 46802
Tel: 260-422-5184, 888-422-5186
E-mail: iloverugs2@aol.com
Website:
www.aaronsorientalruggallery.com

Joseph's Oriental Rug Imports
4230 Fall Creek Parkway North Dr.
Indianapolis, IN 46205
Tel: 317-255-4230
E-mail: info@josephsimports.com
Website: www.josephsimports.com

Sarver's Oriental Rugs
Steven Sarver
Tel: 800-886-3066, 317-255-3066,
mobile 317-695-9826
E-mail: ssarver2@aol.com
Website:
www.sarversorientalrugs.com

Louisiana
Sarouk Shop
Bob Rue
1601 St. Charles Ave.
New Orleans, LA 70130
Tel: 504-522-3260

Maine
William Mor Oriental Rugs
663 Reach Rd.
Deer Isle, ME 04627
Tel: 207-348-2822
E-mail:
rugs@williammororientalrugs.com
Website:
www.williammororientalrugs.com
(Stocks rugs made under the auspices of Cultural Survival)

Tad Runge Oriental Rugs
RFD #1 Box 29A
Yarmouth, ME 04096
Tel: 207-846-9000

Maryland

Hadji Oriental Rugs, Inc.
7135 Wisconsin Ave.
Bethesda, MD 20814-4801
Tel: 301-229-4472

Mark Keshishian & Sons Oriental Carpets
4505 Stanford St.
Chevy Chase, MD 20815
Tel: 301-654-4044
E-mail:
keshishian@orientalcarpets.net
Website: www.orientalcarpets.net

Massachusetts

Antique Rug Gallery, Inc.
195 Belmont St.
Belmont, MA 02478
Tel: 617-489-7531
E-mail:
info@antiqueruggalleryinc.com
Website:
www.antiqueruggalleryinc.com

Bashas Oriental Rugs
Bashir Ahamed
411 Moody St.
Waltham, MA 02154
Tel: 781-642-7333

Beau Ryan's Rare Elements
Beau Ryan
33 Bradford St.
Concord, MA 01742
Tel: 978-318-9299, mobile 617-803-5145
Fax: 978-318-9399
E-mail: beauryan@rareelements.com
Website: www.rareelements.com

D. B. Stock Antique Persian Carpets
Douglas Stock and Helen Stock
464 Washington St.
Wellesley, MA 02482
(781) 237-5859
E-mail: douglas@dbstock.com
Website: www.dbstock.com

Don Barry
Andover MA
Tel: 978-475-8024
E-mail: dbarry@andover.edu

Fine Arts Rug
1475 Beacon St.
Brookline, MA 02446
Tel: 617-731-3733
Fax: 617-566-3713
E-mail: artrugs@bigplanet.com
Website: www.fineartsrug.com

Hassan Oriental Rug Gallery
Richard Hassan
2071 Washington St.
Hanover, MA 02339
Tel: 781-871-0030
E-mail: hassan@tiac.net
Website: www.hassanrugs.com

John J. Collins Jr.
11 Market Sq.
Newburyport, MA 01950
Tel: 978-462-7276
E-mail: info@bijar.com
Website: www.bijar.com
(Collins is an authority on Bidjar carpets and southwest Persian tribal rugs)

Lawrence Kearney
11 Puritan Rd.
Newton Highlands, MA 02461
Tel: 617-964-0012
Fax: 617-964-2982
(By appointment only)

Mario Ratzki Oriental Rugs
40 Charles St.
Boston, MA 02114
Tel: 617-742-7850
Fax: 617-742-8760

Nicholas H. Wright
PO Box 642
Williamstown, MA 01267
Tel: 413-458-5841
E-mail: wrightnh@adelphia.net
(Tibetan rug expert; by appointment only)

Steven King Oriental Rugs
Steven King
1 Design Center Place #614
Boston, MA 02210
Tel: 617-426-3302

Thomas Caruso
76 Beech St.
Belmont, MA 02178
Tel: 617-489-6512

Yayla Tribal Rugs
Chris Walter
283 Broadway
Cambridge, MA 02139
Tel: 617-576-3249
E-mail: yayla@yayla.com
Website: www.yayla.com
(Works with and stocks Cultural
Survival natural-dyed rugs)

Michigan
Azar's Gallery of Oriental Rugs
Azar Alizadeh and Hormoz Alizadeh
670 South Old Woodward
Birmingham, MI 48009
Tel: 248-644-7311, 800-622-RUGS
Fax: 248-644-7314
Website: www.azars.com

Minnesota
Oriental Rug Company, Inc.
Sam Navab, Farzan Navab, and
Ian Grant
911 West 50th St.
Minneapolis, MN 55419
Tel: 612-824-0467
E-mail:
info@orientalrugcompany.com
Website:
www.orientalrugcompany.com
(Special feature: www.orientalrug-
company.com/gazette.htm)

**R. Franklin Hort Oriental Rug
Company**
Ron Hort
3947 Excelsior Blvd., Ste. 107
St. Louis Park, MN 55416
Tel: 952-924-0186

Fax: 952-926-4005
E-mail: ron@hortorientalrugs.com
Website: www.hortorientalrugs.com

Missouri
Bendas Oriental Rugs Co.
Nick Bendas and Dianne Bendas
7505 Delmar Blvd.
St. Louis, MO 63130
Tel: 314-862-4410
Fax: 314-862-4487

Montana
Joseph's Oriental Rugs
Thom Joyce
839 South Higgins
Missoula, MT 59801
Tel: 406-728-8411
E-mail: bruno@afo.net

Nevada
Khyber Pass Rug Co.
George V. Postrozny
230 Evans Ave.
Reno, NV 89501
Tel: 775-786-1050
E-mail: george@intercomm.com

New Hampshire
Asad Khan and Dawn Khan
2 Lebanon St.
Hanover, NH 03755
Tel: 603-643-4008

Oriental Rug Review
Ron O'Callaghan
Sinclair Hill Rd.
New Hampton, NH 03256
Tel: 603-744-9191
E-mail: ronocal@lr.net
Website: www.rugreview.com

Peter Pap Oriental Rugs
Rte. 101, Box 286
Dublin, NH 03444
Tel: 603-563-8717
Fax: 603-563-7158
E-mail: info@peterpap.com
Website: www.peterpap.com
(Exceptional rugs and gallery; see
also under northern California

New Jersey

Ronnie Newman
PO Box 14
Ridgewood, NJ 07451
Tel: 201-825-8775
Fax: 201-825-8719
E-mail: ronnnewman@aol.com
(By appointment only)

New Mexico

Anihita Gallery
Kate Fitzgibbons and Andrew Hale
312 Sandoval St.
Santa Fe, NM 87501
Tel: 505-820-2323
Fax: 505-820-1414

Flying Carpet Fine Rugs and Weavings
Bill Eagleton and Kay Eagleton
208 Ranchitos Rd.
Taos, NM 87571
Tel: 505-751-4035
(Specializes in Kurdish weavings)

Santa Fe Oriental Rugs
Sharon Schenck
212 Galisteo St.
Santa Fe, NM 87501
Tel: 505-982 5152

New York

ABC Carpet Co., Inc.
888 Broadway
New York, NY 10003
Tel: 212-743-3000

Beshar's
1513 1st Ave.
New York, NY 10021
Tel: 212-288-1998
(Quality antique and new oriental rugs)

Doris Leslie Blau Oriental Rugs
15 East 57th St.
New York, NY 10022
Tel: 212-759-3715
(More likely than most to have classical carpets)

Hagop Manoyan
106-15 Queens Blvd. #6A
Forest Hills, NY 11375
Tel: 212-532-4614
E-mail:
h.manoyan@worldnet.att.net
Website: www.cloudband.com/
arcade/hagopmanoyan

Kilim
Linda Miller
150 Thompson St.
New York, NY 10012
Tel: 212-533-1677

Krikor Markarian Oriental Rugs
33 East 33rd St.
New York, NY 10016-5335
Tel: 212-685-1208
Fax: 212-685-1203
(More likely than most to have classical carpets)

Marian Miller Rugs
148 East 28th St., 3rd Fl.
New York, NY 10016
Tel: 212-685-7746
(Kilim specialist)

Mark M. Topalian
281 Fifth Ave., 2nd Fl.
New York, NY 10016
Tel: 212-684-0735
Fax: 212-725-2185
E-mail: topalia@gateway.net

Mark Shilen Gallery
457 Broome St.
New York, NY 10013
Tel: 212-925-3394
Fax: 212-925-1390
E-mail: m.shilen@att.net

Moroccan Rugs and Textiles
Brooke Pickering
Box 37, 1209 Route 213
High Falls, NY 12440
Tel: 914-687-8737
Fax: 914-687-8889.
E-mail: bprugs@aol.com
Website: www.moroccanrugs.com

Thomas J Dwyer Ltd.
304 East Genese St.
Fayetteville, NY 13066
Tel: 315-637-4988

Thos Paddock Oriental Rugs
342 East Ave.
Rochester, NY 14604
Tel: 716-325-3110

North Carolina
Persian Carpet
Bob Fritz and Doug Ley
5634 Chapel Hill Blvd.
Durham, NC 27707
Tel: 919-489-8362
E-mail: perscar@gte.net

Ohio
House of Davidian
John Davidian
7 North Franklin St.
Chagrin Falls, OH 44022
Tel: 216-247-3868
E-mail: info@obannonrugs.com
Website: www.obannonrugs.com

Markarian Oriental Rugs, Inc.
Bill Glasgow, President
3420 Edwards Rd.
Cincinnati, OH 45208
Tel: 513-321-5877

Mousaian's Oriental Rugs
Paul Weaver and Susanne Weaver
1918 Brown St.
Dayton, OH 45409
Tel: 937-223-8088
E-mail: paulweaver@ameritech.net

Oriental Rug Depot
George A. Landis
11471 South Ave.
North Lima, OH 44457
Tel: 216-549-0560

Oregon
James Opie Oriental Rugs, Inc.
1535 Southeast 9th Ave.
Portland, OR 97214
Tel: 503-226-0116
E-mail: info@jamesopie.com
(Expert on southwest Persian tribal
rugs)

Santos Gallery
Mark Santos
521 Southwest 10th Ave.
Portland, OR 97205
Tel: 503-227-6650

Pennsylvania
Jerry Sorkin
155 East Lancaster Ave.
Wayne, PA 19087
Tel: 610-964-0333
Fax: 610-964-0438
E-mail: info@jmsorkin.com
Website: www.jmsorkin.com

Maquam
Dennis Dodds
PO Box 4312
Philadelphia, PA 19118
Tel: 215-848-1182
Fax: 215-848-1189
E-mail: dennisdodds@juno.com
(Exceptional rugs; by appointment
only)

O'Bannon Oriental Carpets
5666 Northumberland St.
Pittsburgh, PA 15217
Tel: 412-422-0300
E-mail: info@obannonrugs.com
Website: www.obannonrugs.com

Peter Scholten Oriental Rugs
117 West Main
Boalsburg, PA 16827
Tel: 814-466-7506
Fax: 814-666-2264

Tennessee
Peter Bruce Oriental Rugs
Peter Bruce Matey
2481 Halle Pkwy.
Collierville, TN 38017
Tel: 901-861-0050
Fax: 901-861-0052
E-mail:
peterbmatey@worldnet.att.net
Website: www.peterbruce.com

Texas
Caravanserai Ltd.
Casey Waller
1435 Dragon St.
Dallas, TX 75207
Tel: 214-741-2131
Fax: 214-741-2137
(Tribal rug specialist)

Istanbul to Samarkand
Donna Endres
Oriental Rugs & Silk Route Artifacts
1101 West 34th St.
Austin, TX 78705
Tel: 512-451-8533
E-mail: dendres@sbcglobal.net

Vermont
Vincent J. Fernandez Oriental Rugs
Rt. 7
Shelburne, VT 05482 (opposite the Shelburne Museum)
Tel: 802-985-2275

Virginia
Ariana Rug Gallery
Jalil Aziz
411 King St.
Alexandria, VA 22314
Tel: 703-683-3206

John & Suzan Wertime
PO Box 16296
Alexandria, VA 22302
Tel: 703-379-8528
E-mail: john.wertime@verizon.net
(Tribal rug and textile experts; by appointment only)

John Murray Oriental Carpets
140 Horseshoe Dr.
Williamsburg, VA 23185
Tel: 804-220-2114

Oriental Rug Gallery, Inc.
Alan R Marschke
687 South Washington St.
Alexandria, VA 22314
Tel: 703-548-0909

Purcell Oriental Rug Co.
Mason Purcell, John Purcell, and Steve Dressel
107 West Main St.
Charlottesville, VA 22902
Tel: 804-971-8822
Fax: 804-971-9346
E-mail: purcell@cstone.net
(Handpicked Afghan Baluch and Turkoman pieces)

Sun Bow Trading Co.
Saul Bardofsky
108 4th St.
Charlottesville, VA 22902
Tel: 804-293-8821

Washington
Driscoll Robbins Oriental Carpets
1002 Western Ave.
Seattle, WA 98104
Tel: 206-292-1115
E-mail: driscoll@nwlink.com
Website: www.driscollrobbins.com
(Focus is on new rugs, including Woven Legends)

Fugio
Keith Pleas
1507 Belmont Ave.
Seattle, WA 98122
Tel: 206-322-6677, 800-571-9590
E-mail: sales@fugio.com
Website: www.fugio.com
(Featuring rugs from the Tibetan and Turkoman natural-dye weaving projects)

J. H. Terry Tribal Rugs
Jon Terry
313A 1st Ave.
South Seattle, WA 98104
Tel: 206-233-9766
Fax: 206-621-0831

Wisconsin
Bogosian Carpets
11005 West Bluemound Rd.
Milwaukee, WI 53226
Tel: 414-774-8540

Wyoming
Davies Reid
Heidi Davies and Terry Reid
15 East Deloney Ave.
Jackson, WY 83001
Tel: 307-739-1009
Fax: 307-739-1019
Website: www.daviesreid.com

DEALERS IN NATURAL-DYE RUGS

Kilim.com handles superior natural-dye rugs but offers them only through a website that is very much worth browsing through.

E-mail: info@kilim.com
Website: www.kilim.com

DOBAG Rugs
Primary Source
Return to Tradition
Bill McDonnell
3319 Sacramento St.
San Francisco, CA 94118
Tel: 415-921-4180
E-mail: rugs@dobag.com
Website: www.returntotradition.com

Other Sources
Shaver-Ramsey Oriental Rugs
Paul Ramsey and Carolyn Shaver
2414 East 3rd Ave.
Denver, CO 80206
Tel: 303-320-6363

Fax: 303-320-1541
E-mail: info@shaver-ramsey.com
Website: www.shaver-ramsey.com

Woven Legends
Primary Source
Woven Legends
4700 Wissahickon Ave.
Philadelphia, PA 19144
Tel: 215-849-8344
Website: www.wovenlegends.com

Material Culture
4700 Wissahickon Avenue
Philadelphia, PA 19144
Tel: 215-849-8030
E-mail: info@materialculture.com
Website: www.materialculture.com

Other Sources
Too many to list. Browse the colorful Woven Legends website, then call or e-mail the listed dealers nearest you.

Yayla Tribal Rugs/ Cultural Survival
Primary Source
Yayla Tribal Rugs
Chris Walter
283 Broadway
Cambridge, MA 02139
Tel: 617-576-3249
E-mail: yayla@yayla.com
Website: www.yayla.com

Other Sources
William Mor Oriental Rugs
663 Reach Road
Deer Isle, ME 04627
Tel: 207-348-2822
E-mail:
rugs@williammororientalrugs.com
Website:
www.williammororientalrugs.com

Emmett Eiland Oriental Rug Co.
1326 9th St.
Berkeley, CA 94710
Tel: 510-526-1087, 888-811-7847
E-mail: erugs@internetrugs.com
Website: www.internetrugs.com

Orient Rugs
168 Sanchez at Market
San Francisco, CA 94114
Tel: 415-552-2511
Website: www.orientrugs.com

Fugio
Keith Pleas
1507 Belmont Ave.
Seattle, WA 98122
Tel: 800-571-9590
E-mail: sales@fugio.com
Website: www.fugio.com

Nomad Rugs
Christopher Wahlgren
3775 24th St.
San Francisco, CA 94114
Tel: 415-401-8833
Fax: 415-401-8855
E-mail: christopher@nomadrugs.com
Website: www.nomadrugs.com

JOURNALS AND PERIODICALS

Ghereh: International Carpet & Textile Review
Taher Sabahi
E-mail: Ghereh@tin.it
Website: www.ghereh.com
(1 year, 6 issues, $150)

HALI Publications Ltd.
St Giles House
50 Poland Street,
London W1F 7AX, UK
E-mail: hali@centaur.co.uk
Website:
www.subscription.co.uk/help/centaur
(International coverage of rugs and
textiles; well printed in exceptional
color; 1 year, 6 issues, $156)

Textile Museum Journal
2320 South St. NW
Washington, DC 20008
Tel: 202-667-0441
Website: www.textilemuseum.org
(The *TMJ* was an annual, but it now
seems to come out on a less regu-
lar basis)

NOTABLE RUG COLLECTIONS

Museums
Hours and open days are subject to change, so please call before visiting.

Art Institute of Chicago
111 South Michigan Ave.
Chicago, IL 60603
Tel: 313-443-3600
Website: www.artic.edu

Cleveland Museum of Art
University Circle 11150 East Blvd.
Cleveland, OH 44106
Tel: 216-421-7340
E-mail: info@clevelandart.org
Website: www.clevelandart.org

The deYoung Museum
2501 Irving Street
San Francisco, CA 94122-1514
Tel: 415-863-3330 (24-hour hotline)

Fogg Art Museum
32 Quincy St.
Cambridge, MA 02139
Tel: 617-495-9400
Website: www.artmuseums.har-
vard.edu

George V. W. Smith Art Museum
222 State St.
Springfield, MA 01103
Tel: 413-733-4214

Indianapolis Museum of Art
4000 Michigan Rd.
Indianapolis, IN 46208

Tel: 317-920-2660
E-mail: ima@ima-art.org
Website: www.ima-art.org
(Home of the Boucher Baluch Collection)

Los Angeles County Museum of Art
5905 Wilshire Blvd.
Los Angeles, CA 90036
Tel: 323-857-6000
Website: www.lacma.org

Maltwood Art Museum & Gallery
University of Victoria
Victoria, BC V8W 3P2
Tel: 250-721-8298
Website: www.maltwood.uvic.ca

Metropolitan Museum of Art
1000 5th Ave. at 82nd St.
New York, NY 10028
Tel: 212-535-7710 (recorded information)
(Note that the Islamic Galleries, in which the museum's oriental rug collection is displayed, closed on June 2, 2003, for a three-year renovation project)

Middle East Institute
1761 North St. NW
Washington, DC 20036
Tel: 202-785-1141
Website: www.midesti.org

Philadelphia Museum of Art
26th St. and Benjamin Franklin Pkwy.
Philadelphia, PA 19130
Tel: 215-763-8100
Website: www.philamuseum.org

Textile Museum
2320 South St. NW
Washington, DC 20008
Tel: 202-667-0441
Website: www.textilemuseum.org
(Holds exhibits, an annual conference, and rug and textile appreciation sessions on Saturday mornings, and has a gift shop and an extensive library)

Textile Museum of Canada
55 Centre Ave.
Toronto, ON M5G 2H5
Tel: 416-599-5321
E-mail: info@textilemuseum.ca
Website: www.museumfortextiles.on.ca

Victoria and Albert Museum
Cromwell Road, South Kensington
London SW7 2RL UK
Website: www.vam.ac.uk

Other Collections:
California
Yosemite National Park: The Persian flat weaves in the Ahwahnee Hotel
North Carolina
Asheville: The Biltmore Estate
New Bern: Tryon Palace Restoration
Pennsylvania
Bryn Athyn: Glencairn Museum
Virginia
Williamsburg: The Williamsburg Restoration

ORIENTAL RUG BOOKS

Many of the books listed below may be obtainable only from specialist dealers, the names of which will be found at the conclusion of the list. Rug books tend to be very expensive; all of the listed books are well regarded and can, with a few exceptions, be found for less than $100.

General Rug Books
The three rug books no collector should be without are:

Eiland, Murray L., Jr., and Murray Eiland III. *Oriental Carpets: A Complete Guide.*
Boston 1998. Hardcover. 9 × 12. 294 pages. 330 color photos.

15 maps, 20 diagrams. Revised (4th ed.) updated classic with all color plates.

Ford, P. R. J. *Oriental Carpet Design: A Guide to Traditional Motifs, Patterns, and Symbols.*
New York 1992. Stiff paperback with flaps. 9.5 × 12.75. 352 pages. 400 color illustrations, 400 black and white illustrations. 14 maps.

Thompson, Jon. *Carpets from the Tents, Cottages and Workshops of Asia.*
London 1993. Stiff paperback. 8.5 × 11. 176 pages. 114 color illustrations, 8 black and white illustrations. 2 maps.

Baluch

Boucher, Jeff. *Baluchi Woven Treasures.*
London 1989 (1996). Hardcover. 8.5 × 11. 152 pp. 63 color photos. 2nd edition.

Caucasus

Burns, James. *The Caucasus: Traditions in Weaving.*
Seattle 1987. Hardcover. 12 × 9. 74 pages. 67 color photos. Distinguished pile and flat-woven collection.

Ellis, Charles Grant. *Early Caucasian Rugs.*
Washington, DC, 1975. Paperback. 8.5 × 11. 112 pages.16 color photos, 21 black and white illustrations. Important Textile Museum exhibition catalog.

Eder, Doris. *Orientteppiche Band 1 Kaukasische Teppiche.*
Munchen 1990. Hardcover. 10 × 9. 432 pages. 350 color photos. German text but many pictures.

Chinese

Eiland, Murray L. *Chinese and Exotic Rugs.*
Boston 1979. Hardcover. 8.5 × 11. 246 pages. 52 color photos, 180 black and white illustrations. 30 drawings. Includes Tibetan, Mongolian, East Turkestan, Indian, North African, and Balkan rugs.

Contemporary Collectible Rugs

Eiland, Emmett. *Oriental Rugs Today: A Guide to the Best in New Carpets from the East.*
Berkeley, CA, 2000. Paperback. 8.5 × 11.200 pages. Many color plates.

East Turkestan

Bidder, Hans. *Carpets from East Turkestan: Known As Khotan, Samarkand and Kansu Carpets.*
London 1964 (1979). Hardcover. 8 × 10. 96 pages. 20 color photos, 50 black and white illustrations.

India

Walker, Daniel. *Flowers Underfoot: Indian Carpets of the Mughal Era.*
New York 1997. Hardcover. 9 × 12. 220 pages. 108 color photos. Catalog of Metropolitan Museum of Art exhibition of sixteenth- and seventeenth-century carpets.

Iran/Persia

Collins, John J., Jr. *Flowers of the Desert.*
Newburyport, MA, 1987. Paperback. 8.5 × 11. 54 pages. 50 color photos. Dealer exhibition of south Persian tribal rugs.

MacDonald, Brian W. *Tribal Rugs: Treasures of the Black Tent.* Woodbridge, UK, 1997. Hardcover. 8.5 × 11. 302 pages. 220 color photos. Persian tribal and village rugs.

Opie, James. *Tribal Rugs of Southern Persia.* Portland, OR, 1981. Hardcover. 8.5 × 11. 224 pages. 100 color photos. Very good color photos.

Tanavoli, Parvis. *Persian Flatweaves.* Woodbridge, UK, 2002. Hardcover. 8 × 11. 350 pages. 244 color photos, 198 black and white illustrations. Survey of antique kilim floor covers and hangings.

Edwards, A. Cecil. *The Persian Carpet.* London 1953 (1983). Hardcover. 9 × 11. 384 pages. 4 color photos, 419 black and white illustrations. Expensive and lacking in color photos, but a standard text on this subject.

Tibet

Kuloy, Hallvard Kare. *Tibetan Rugs.* Bangkok 1982 (1995). Paperback. 7.5 × 8.5. 235 pages. 259 color photos. Extensively illustrated.

Turkoman

Hoffmeister, Peter. *Turcoman Carpets in Franconia.* Edinburgh 1980. Paperback. 9 × 12.5. 105 pages. 60 color photos. Noted collection of early Turkoman rugs.

Mackie, Louise W., and Jon Thompson. *Turkmen Tribal Carpets and Tradition.* Washington, DC, 1980. Hardcover. 9 × 12. 240 pages. 95 color photos, 117 black and white illustrations. A Textile Museum exhibition catalog of rugs from private collections.

Pinner, Robert, and Murray L. Eiland Jr. *Between the Black Desert and the Red: Turkmen Carpets from the Weidersberg Collection.* San Francisco 1999. Paperback. 9 × 12. 144 pages. 100 color photos, 50 black and white illustrations A museum exhibition catalog of an outstanding private collection.

Turkey

Aslanapa, Oktay. *One Thousand Years of Turkish Carpets.* Istanbul 1988. Hardcover. 8 × 11. 240 pages. 162 color photos, 86 black and white illustrations.

Zipper, Kurt, and C. Fritzsche. *Oriental Rugs: Volume 4 Turkish.* Munich (Suffolk) 1989 (1995). Hardcover. 8.5 × 10. 250 pages. 275 color photos. Introductory book with antique and contemporary examples. From the Antique Collectors Club.

Flatwoven Rugs

Acar, Belkis Balpinar. *Zilim-Cicim-Zili-Soumak: Turkish Flatweaves.* Istanbul 1983. Hardcover. 8 × 11. 128 pages. 30 color photos. A basic work on Turkish flat weaves.

Justin, Valerie. *Flat-Woven Rugs of the World: Kelim, Soumak and Brocading.* New York 1980. Hardcover. 9 × 12. 224 pages. 59 color, 250 black and white illustrations. Very good reference book for flat weaves of the world.

Rug Structure, Repair, and Dyes

Mallett, Marla. *Woven Structures: A Guide to Oriental Rug and Textile Analysis.*
Atlanta, GA, 1998 (2000). Paperback. 8.5 × 11. 188 pages. 490 black and white illustrations. Revised edition. Pioneering research clearly conveyed.

Stone, Peter. *Oriental Rug Repair.* Buchanan, MI, 2000. Paperback. 8.5 × 11. 184 pages. 296 black and white illustrations.. Revised and expanded edition. Comprehensive guide to the repair, cleaning, and care of oriental rugs.

Bohmer, Harald. *Koekboya: Natural Dyes and Textiles.* Ganderkese, Germany, 2002. Hardcover. 8.5 × 11. 298 pages. 300 color photos. A color journey from Turkey to India and beyond.

ORIENTAL RUG INTERNET WEBSITES

www.acor-rugs.org
www.cloudband.com
www.icoc-orientalrugs.org
www.jozan.net
www.marlamallett.com, which includes an annotated list of links to rug-related sites
www.rugnews.com
www.rugreview.com
www.spongobongo.com
www.tukotec.com
www.world-rugs.com

ORIENTAL RUG ORGANIZATIONS AND SOCIETIES

American Conference on Oriental Rugs

The American Conference on Oriental Rugs (ACOR) is a nonprofit organization established to promote the understanding and appreciation of oriental rugs and textiles through its biannual conferences and its member rug and textile societies throughout North America.

Every two years, ACOR sponsors a three-day conference in a major U.S. city for the continued advancement of, and education about, oriental rugs and textiles. The first conference was held in Boston, Massachusetts, in 1992. ACOR 7 was held in Seattle, Washington, in March 2004.

ACOR conferences feature approximately twenty-eight one-hour focus sessions addressing a wide variety of subjects of interest to collectors, dealers, academics, and enthusiasts that comprise the "rug world." The subjects are diverse, ranging from general surveys of tribal and village rug and textile groups, to specialized exploration of subjects such as carpet identification, rug restoration, textile esthetics, effects of light, natural dyes, design origins, and rug books.

A central feature is the bazaar-like setting where dealers display fine antique carpets and textiles. The conferences are accompanied by memorable exhibitions at various museums, art centers, and rug dealers within the host city.

For more information, consult the ACOR website at www.acor-rugs.org.

Directory of ACOR Member Societies

Arizona Oriental Rug/Textile Association (AZ)
Contact: Sally Komerska
Tel: 520-323-0320
E-mail:
s.komerska@worldnet.att.net

Armenian Rugs Society (AR)
Contact: James Keshishian
Tel: 301-654-4044
Fax: 301-907-8236
E-mail jkesh@msn.com
Website:
www.armenianrugssociety.com

Central Florida Rug Society (CF)
Contact: Doug Connor
Tel: 813-643-2377
E-mail: dconnor@pd10.state.fl.us

Chicago Rug Society (CH)
Contact: Suzanne Kaufman
Tel: 815-963-6543
Fax: 815-963-6543
E-mail:
suzannekaufman@msn.com

Cleveland Rug Society (CL)
Contact: Joan Long
Tel: 330-666-4876
E-mail: jcl.ebl@att.net

Colorado Textile Group (CO)
Contact: Richard Stewart
Tel: 303-444-3720
Fax: 303-443-7712
E-mail:
Richard_Stewart@webTV.net

Gesellschaft der Freunde Islamischer Kunst und Kultur (GF)
Contact: Christian Erber
Tel: 011-49-89-7673-6360
E-mail: erber@erber-statik.de
Website:
www.freunde-islamischer-kunst.de

Hajji Baba Club (HB)
Contact: Joseph Doherty
Tel: 212-979-7013
Fax: 212-979-7127
E-mail: jdoherty@mackenziepartners.com
Website: www.hajjibaba.org

International Hajji Baba Society (IH)
Contact: Wendel Swan
Tel: 703-960-0343
Fax: 703-683-7545
E-mail: wdswan@erols.com

Kansas City Oriental Rug and Textile Association (KC)
Contact: Carol Mundy
Tel: 913-362-2006
Fax: 913-362-0701
E-mail: camundy@mindspring.com
Website: www.kcorta.org

Montreal Oriental Rug Society (MO)
Contact: Ian McLaren
Tel: 514-521-7433
Fax: 514-522-3013
E-mail: imclaren@grandnord.ca

New Calgary Rug and Textile Club (NC)
Contact: Jean Landa
Tel: 403-270-2880
Fax: 403-270-3030
E-mail: landa@acs.ucalgary.ca

New England Rug Society (NE)
Contact: Mark Hopkins
Tel: 781-259-9444
Fax: 781-259-1529
E-mail: mopkins@netway.com
Website: www.ne-rugsociety.org

Philadelphia Oriental Rug Society (PH)
Contact: Samy Rabinovic
Tel: 215-860-8869
Fax: 215-860-7779
E-mail: rabinovic@aol.com
Website: www.geocities.com/jbulyk

Portland Area Rug Society (PO)
Contact: Leslie Atiyeh
Tel: 503-538-7560
Fax: 503-538-8239
E-mail: pars@atiyeh.com

Princeton Rug Society (PR)
Contact: Jeffrey K. McVey
Tel: 609-397-1326
E-mail: lamfellow@yahoo.com

Quebec Oriental Rug and Textile Society (QU)
Contact: Janice Summers
Tel: 514-288-1218
Fax: 514-288-1210
E-mail: araratrug@videotron.ca

Rug Society of San Diego (RS)
Contact: Ray Rosenberg
Tel: 619-291-4275, 603-536-2990
Fax: 619-297-8240
E-mail: rugbuff@aol.com

Rug and Textile Society of Indiana (RT)
Contact: Erik Risman
Tel: 317-873-0012
Fax: 317-733-1278
E-mail: err1@comcast.net

St. Louis Oriental Rug & Textile Association (SL)
Contact: Tom Hubbard
Tel: 636-530-6140
E-mail: tphubb@swbell.net

San Francisco Bay Area Rug Society (SB)
Contact: Peter Poullada
Tel: 415-602-0709
E-mail: sppoull@aol.com
Website: www.sfbars.org

Seattle Textile and Rug Society (SE)
Contact: Fred Ingham
Tel: 206-325-8907
Fax: 206-325-8907
E-mail: fingham@yahoo.com

Teppichfreunde (TE)
Contact: Dr. Herbert J. Exner
Tel: 011-49-51-30-8771
Fax: 011-49-51-30-8871
E-mail: exner-wedemark@t-online.de

Textile Group of Los Angeles (TGLAinc) (TG)
Contact: Brian Morehouse
Tel: 323-931-4987
Fax: 323-931-4987
E-mail: morehousebri@aol.com

Textile Museum Associates of Southern Cal. (TA)
Contact: Val Arbab
Tel: 858-453-4686
Fax: 858-457-3647
E-mail: valarbab@att.net

Textile and Oriental Rug Club of Houston (HO)
Contact: Alan Garrison
Tel: 713-524-1643
E-mail: agarriso@wt.net

Toronto Oriental Rug Society (TO)
Contact: Katharine Green
Tel: 905-471-7381, 301-897-2137
E-mail: 1463@compuserve.com

Triangle Rug Society (TR)
Contact: Lucille Kimble
Tel: 919-489-2702
E-mail: kimble@psych.duke.edu

International Conference on Oriental Carpets

The International Conference on Oriental Carpets (ICOC) "is dedicated to advancing the understanding of carpet and related textile arts, primarily of the eastern hemisphere."

To this end, the ICOC arranges periodic international forums to present papers and exhibitions intended to encourage the exchange of knowledge and theories about oriental carpets and publishes conference papers, exhibition catalogs, and other materials.

The 2005 ICOC conference will be held in Istanbul, Turkey. A regional conference will be held in Sydney, Australia, in September 2004. Details may be found at www.icoc-orientalrugs.org.

RUG BOOK DEALERS

The East-West Room
Myrna Bloom
3139 Alpin Dr.
Dresher, PA 19025
Tel: 215-657-0178
Fax: 215-657-6685
Website: www.myrnabloom.com

IranBooks
6931 Wisconsin Ave.
Bethesda, MD 20815
Tel: 301-986-0079
Fax: 301-987-8707
Website: iranbook@ix.netcom.com

Dennis B. Marquand Oriental Rug and Textile Books
PO Box 1187
Culver City, CA 90232
Tel: 310-313-0177
E-mail: dmarquand@rugbooks.com
Website: www.rugbooks.com

The Rug Book Shop
Paul Kreiss
2603 Talbot Rd.
Baltimore, MD 21216
Tel: 410-367-8194 (evenings and weekends)
E-mail: enquiries@rugbookshop.com
Website: www.RugBookShop.com

Textile Museum
2320 South St. NW
Washington, DC 20008
Tel: 202-667-0441
Website: www.textilemuseum.org
(Museum members receive a discount)

TOURS OF INTEREST TO RUG COLLECTORS

Samy Rabinovic
Newtown, PA 18940
Tel: 215-860-8869
Fax: 215-860-7779
E-mail: centralasiatours@aol.com
Website: www.centralasiatours.com
(Excellent reputation for tours)
Note that tours are also periodically offered through the Textile Museum and the Smithsonian Institution.

THE INSTANT
EXPERT QUIZ

1. Name five countries where the production of hand-knotted rugs is an important industry.

2. What three qualities must a rug possess to be considered collectible?

3. In which country did the revival of the use of natural dyes originate?

4. Why is it important to overcast the ends of rugs?

5. What American association holds biennial conferences aided by its member rug societies?

6. Why should the backs of wall-hung rugs be periodically inspected?

7. Why should rugs with cotton foundations never be stored in damp areas?

8. What are the chief disadvantages of buying rugs at auction?

9. Should rugs be wrapped in plastic for storage?

10. What is the distinguishing characteristic of a genuine oriental rug?

11. Does the fineness of knotting characterize a collectible rug?

12. What is gained in terms of decorative value and wearability when a pile rug's knot count exceeds 400 per square inch?

13. What is the name of the popular motif that resembles a pear with a bent top?

14. What popular class of antique collectible rugs is being faked cleverly enough to fool experienced dealers?

15. Can both silk rugs and wool rugs be cleaned by washing?

16. Is painting a rug to disguise wear ever permissible?

17. Rugs wear better when an underlayment is provided, but in what circumstance is an underlayment essential?

Answers

1. Iran, Turkey, India, China, Pakistan, Afghanistan, Romania, Egypt

2. a. Clarity of color derived from natural sources, b. relationship between size of rug and elements within it, c. selection and spacing of motifs

3. Turkey

4. To prevent the loss of wefts and the knots protected by them.

5. ACOR—The American Conference on Oriental Rugs

6. To see if moths or their larvae have taken up residence.

7. Cotton, a cellulose fiber, is subject to dry rot, which is irreversible.

8. No returns or exchanges are possible.

9. No.

10. The weaving and knotting is done by hand.

11. No. Many valuable collectible pieces are coarsely knotted.

12. Nothing.

13. Boteh

14. Caucasian

15. No. Silk rugs, as well as wool rugs with a high percentage of silk in the pile, should always be dry-cleaned by an experienced professional.

16. Only if you own it and painting might allow a favorite old rug a few more years of decorative life.

17. When a lightweight rug is placed on a smooth or polished floor.

INDEX